# Sportographica

Sportog

# raphica

Martin & Simon Toseland

Quercus

# Contents

# Early Olympic sports

Events from earlier Olympics that haven't survived
and the nations who won gold

**LIVE PIGEON
SHOOTING**
1900 Belgium

**ROPE CLIMB**
1896 Greece
1904 USA
1906 Greece
1924 Czechoslovakia
1932 USA

**UNDERWATER SWIMMING RACE**
1900 France

**REAL TENNIS**
1908 USA

**ONE-HANDED
WEIGHT LIFTING**
1896 GB

**TUG OF WAR**
1904 USA
1906 Germany
1908 GB
1912 Sweden
1920 GB

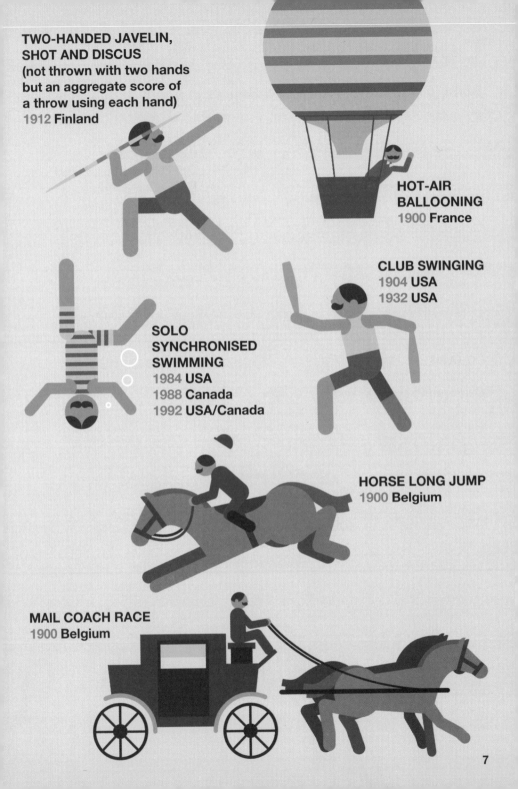

**TWO-HANDED JAVELIN, SHOT AND DISCUS**
(not thrown with two hands but an aggregate score of a throw using each hand)
1912 Finland

**HOT-AIR BALLOONING**
1900 France

**CLUB SWINGING**
1904 USA
1932 USA

**SOLO SYNCHRONISED SWIMMING**
1984 USA
1988 Canada
1992 USA/Canada

**HORSE LONG JUMP**
1900 Belgium

**MAIL COACH RACE**
1900 Belgium

# Duck!

## Some of the fastest recorded objects in sport

**BADMINTON**
206.00mph / 331.52kph
Fu Haifeng 2005

**SQUASH**
175.00mph / 281.64kph
Cameron Pilley 2011

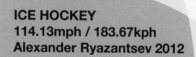

**ICE HOCKEY**
114.13mph / 183.67kph
Alexander Ryazantsev 2012

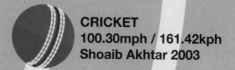

**CRICKET**
100.30mph / 161.42kph
Shoaib Akhtar 2003

**GOLF**
211.00mph / 339.57kph
Maurice Allen 2012

**JAI ALAI**
188.00mph / 302.56kph
José Ramón Areitio 1979

**TENNIS**
163.40mph / 262.97kph
Samuel Groth 2012

**FOOTBALL**
114.00mph / 183.47kph
David Hirst 1996

**BASEBALL**
108.10mph / 173.97kph
Nolan Ryan 1974

# New balls, please!

The longest professional tennis matches in history

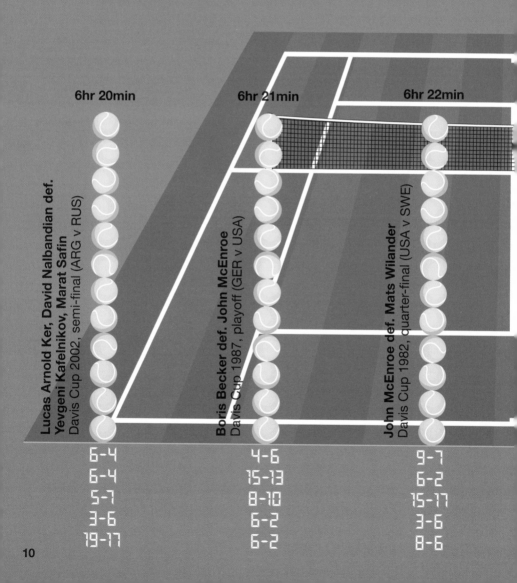

**6hr 20min**

Lucas Arnold Ker, David Nalbandian def.
Yevgeni Kafelnikov, Marat Safin
Davis Cup 2002, semi-final (ARG v RUS)

6-4
6-4
5-7
3-6
19-17

**6hr 21min**

Boris Becker def. John McEnroe
Davis Cup 1987, playoff (GER v USA)

4-6
15-13
8-10
6-2
6-2

**6hr 22min**

John McEnroe def. Mats Wilander
Davis Cup 1982, quarter-final (USA v SWE)

9-7
6-2
15-17
3-6
8-6

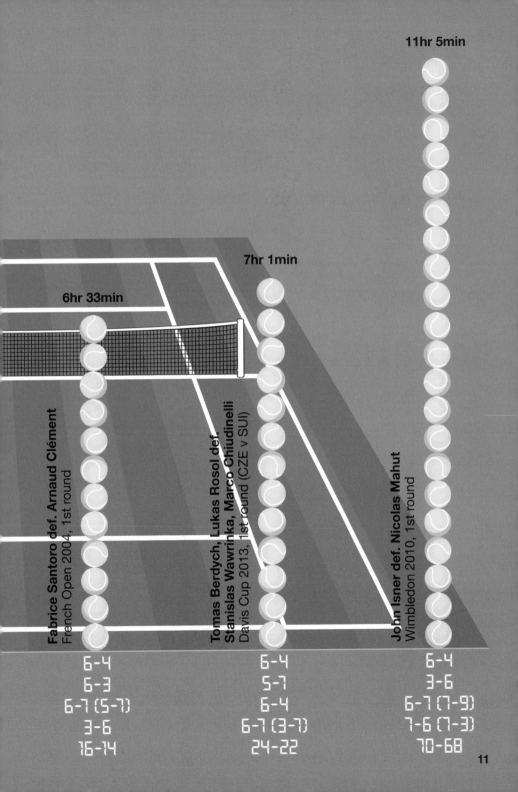

11hr 5min

7hr 1min

6hr 33min

**Fabrice Santoro def. Arnaud Clément**
French Open 2004, 1st round

**Tomas Berdych, Lukas Rosol def.**
**Stanislas Wawrinka, Marco Chiudinelli**
Davis Cup 2013, 1st round (CZE v SUI)

**John Isner def. Nicolas Mahut**
Wimbledon 2010, 1st round

| 6-4 | 6-4 | 6-4 |
| 6-3 | 5-7 | 3-6 |
| 6-7 (5-7) | 6-4 | 6-7 (7-9) |
| 3-6 | 6-7 (3-7) | 7-6 (7-3) |
| 16-14 | 24-22 | 70-68 |

# Fleeing the avalanche

## The fastest ways to move on snow and ice

Speed skating
54.2kph (33.7mph)

Polar bear
40kph (24mph)

Speed skiing
251.4kph (156.2mph)

Downhill skiing
155.5kph (96.6mph)

4-man bobsleigh
153kph (95.1mph)

Skeleton sled
146.6kph (91.1mph)

Luge
139.9kph (86.9mph)

# Formula young

The twenty youngest Formula One World Drivers Championship winners ranked by age on the date they won the title

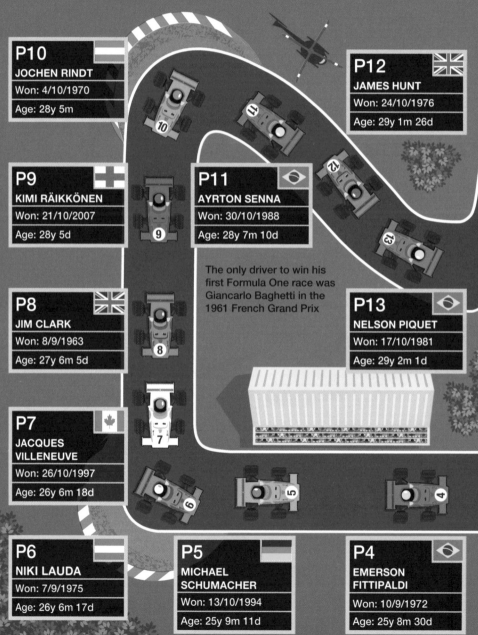

**P10**
JOCHEN RINDT
Won: 4/10/1970
Age: 28y 5m

**P12**
JAMES HUNT
Won: 24/10/1976
Age: 29y 1m 26d

**P9**
KIMI RÄIKKÖNEN
Won: 21/10/2007
Age: 28y 5d

**P11**
AYRTON SENNA
Won: 30/10/1988
Age: 28y 7m 10d

The only driver to win his first Formula One race was Giancarlo Baghetti in the 1961 French Grand Prix

**P8**
JIM CLARK
Won: 8/9/1963
Age: 27y 6m 5d

**P13**
NELSON PIQUET
Won: 17/10/1981
Age: 29y 2m 1d

**P7**
JACQUES VILLENEUVE
Won: 26/10/1997
Age: 26y 6m 18d

**P6**
NIKI LAUDA
Won: 7/9/1975
Age: 26y 6m 17d

**P5**
MICHAEL SCHUMACHER
Won: 13/10/1994
Age: 25y 9m 11d

**P4**
EMERSON FITTIPALDI
Won: 10/9/1972
Age: 25y 8m 30d

## P14
**MIKE HAWTHORN**
Won: 19/10/1958
Age: 29y 6m 10d

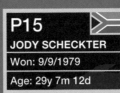

## P15
**JODY SCHECKTER**
Won: 9/9/1979
Age: 29y 7m 12d

## P16
**MIKA HÄKKINEN**
Won: 1/11/1998
Age: 30y 1m 5d

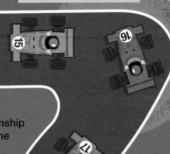

The oldest World Championship winning driver was Argentine Juan Manuel Fangio, who won the 1957 championship, his fifth title, at the age of 46 years and 41 days

## P17
**JACKIE STEWART**
Won: 7/9/1969
Age: 30y 2m 28d

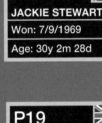

## P18
**ALAIN PROST**
Won: 6/10/1985
Age: 30y 7m 13d

## P19
**JOHN SURTEES**
Won: 25/10/1964
Age: 30y 8m 15d

## P20
**DENNY HULME**
Won: 22/10/1967
Age: 31y 4m 5d

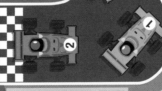

## P3
**FERNANDO ALONSO**
Won: 25/9/2005
Age: 24y 1m 28d

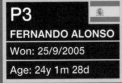

## P2
**LEWIS HAMILTON**
Won: 2/11/2008
Age: 23y 9m 27d

## P1
**SEBASTIAN VETTEL**
Won: 14/11/2010
Age: 23y 4m 12d

# Throwing their weight around

**The most common winning moves in Sumo wrestling**

## TSUKIOTOSHI

The wrestler pushes his opponent down out of the ring onto his back with a hard thrust or shove

## UWATENAGE

The wrestler grabs his opponent's mawashi (belt) by extending his arm over his opponent's arm and throws him to the ground while turning sideways

## SHITATENAGE

The wrestler grabs his opponent's mawashi by extending his arm under his opponent's arm, then turns sideways and throws the opponent down to the ground

## UWATEDASHINAGE

The wrestler grabs his opponent's mawashi by extending his arm over his opponent's arm or back while pulling them forwards to the ground

## YORIKIRI

The wrestler holds the opponent's mawashi and forces him backwards out of the ring

## ABISETAOSHI

The wrester forces his opponent down on to his back by leaning forward while grappling

## OSHIDASHI

The wrestler pushes his opponent out of the ring without holding the mawashi or fully extending his arms. Hand contact must be maintained throughout the push

## OSHITAOSHI

As Oshidashi above, but the opponent falls on his back at the end of the move

## YORITAOSHI

As Yorikiri above, but the opponent collapses on his back at the end of the move

17

# Reach for the stars

## The tallest athletes ever to have competed in different sports

**Edouard Beaupré**
2.51m (8ft 3in)
Canada
Wrestler

**Gheorghe Mureșan**
2.31m (7ft 7in)
Romania
Joint tallest basketball
player

**Manute Bol**
2.31m (7ft 7in)
Sudan
Joint tallest
basketball player

**Dmitriy Muserskiy**
2.18m (7ft 2in)
Russia
Volleyball player

**Mohammad Irfan**
2.16m (7ft 1in)
Pakistan
Cricketer

**Aaron Sandilands**
2.11m (6ft 11in)
Australia
Joint tallest player in
Australian rules
football

**Peter Street**
2.11m (6ft 11in)
Australia
Joint tallest player in
Australian rules
football

**Rolandas Gimbutis**
2.09m (6ft 10in)
Lithuania
Olympic
swimmer

**Ivo Karlović**
2.08m (6ft 10in)
Croatia
Tallest tennis player
on the ATP Tour

**Zdeno Chára**
2.06m (6ft 9in)
Slovakia
Tallest player in
National Hockey
League

**Richard Metcalfe**
2.13m (7ft 0in)
United Kingdom
Tallest rugby union
player

**Ted van der Parre**
2.13m (7ft 0in)
Netherlands
Tallest World's
Stongest Man

**Richard Sligh**
2.13m (7ft 0in)
United States
NFL player

**Nikolai Valuev**
2.13m (7ft 0in)
Russia
Tallest world
champion in
heavyweight boxing

**Jon Rauch**
2.11m (6ft 11in)
United States
Baseball

**Ingo Schultz**
2.01m (6ft 7in)
Germany
Sprinter

**Velichko Cholakov**
2.01m (6ft 7in)
Bulgaria
Olympic weightlifter

**Phil Blackmar**
2.01m (6ft 7in)
United States
Tallest golfer on
the PGA Tour

**Peter Crouch**
2.01m (6ft 7in)
United Kingdom
Footballer

# Plain sailing

## The 7 classes of yacht race in the Olympics

**FINN**
Men's single-handed with mast to the front. One of the oldest continuously picked categories of Olympic sailing boat. Name comes from inaugural selection for Helsinki Games in 1952

**49er**
Two-handed skiff. Name comes from length of hull (4.99m)

**470**
Double-handed, single hull. Name is from length of hull (4.7m)

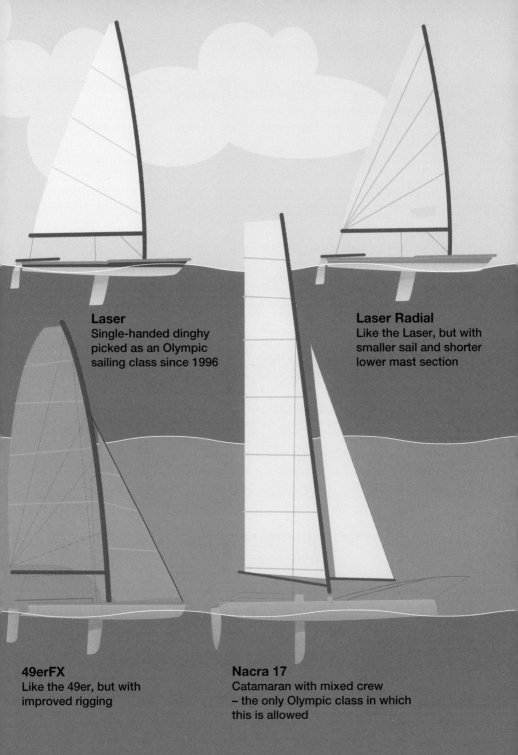

**Laser**
Single-handed dinghy picked as an Olympic sailing class since 1996

**Laser Radial**
Like the Laser, but with smaller sail and shorter lower mast section

**49erFX**
Like the 49er, but with improved rigging

**Nacra 17**
Catamaran with mixed crew – the only Olympic class in which this is allowed

# Sporting Oscars

Which sports have featured most frequently
in film's hall of fame?

**CYCLING**

Breaking Away
1979

**AMERICAN
FOOTBALL**

Jerry Maguire 1996
The Blind Side 2010

**ATHLETICS**

Chariots of Fire
1987

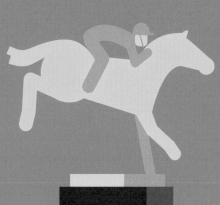

## HORSE RACING

National Velvet
1944

## POOL

The Color of Money 1986
The Hustler 1961

## BASEBALL

Pride of the Yankees
1942

## BOXING

The Fighter 2010
Million Dollar Baby 2004
Raging Bull 1980
Rocky 1976
Champion 1950
The Champ 1931

# Baffling the batter

Trajectories of the most popular baseball pitches

## FASTBALLS

**Four-seam fastball:** fastest pitch with little or no lateral or vertical movement

**Two-seam fastball:** slower than the four-seam but still fast. The ball curves slightly down and in the direction of the pitcher's dominant side

**Cutter:** moves towards the pitcher's glove hand; not as fast as a fastball but faster than a slider

**Splitter:** like a fastball but drops off suddenly at end of pitch

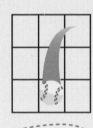

**Forkball:** like a splitter, looks like a fastball but drops off at the end due to topspin rather than backspin

# BREAKING BALLS

**Curveball:** doesn't actually curve but drops in a 12 o'clock to 6 o'clock trajectory. Slower than a fastball

**Slider:** typically breaks from 9 o'clock to 3 o'clock; faster than a curveball

**Slurve:** combines a slider and a curveball; like a curveball but with more lateral movement

**Screwball:** a slider or curveball that breaks in the opposite direction

# CHANGEUPS

**Changeup:** thrown like a fastball but actually 10–15mph (16–24kph) slower, causing batter to swing too early

**Palmball:** variation of the changeup but slower

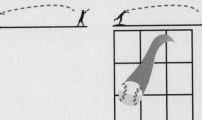

**Circle changeup:** slower pitch mimics the screwball but much slower delivery

# Europe vs USA

## Facts and figures about the Ryder Cup

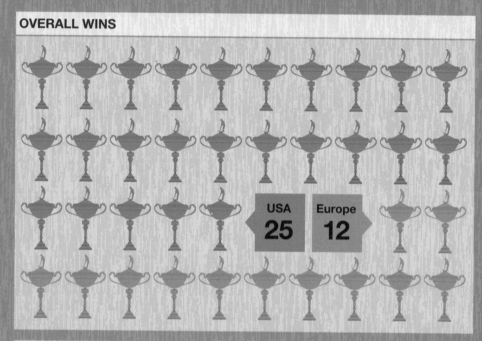

### OVERALL WINS

| USA | Europe |
|-----|--------|
| 25  | 12     |

### HOLES WON

|         | SINGLES | FOURSOME | FOURBALLS |
|---------|---------|----------|-----------|
| USA     | 224     | 131      | 86        |
| Europe  | 160     | 99       | 76        |
| Halved  | 62      | 27       | 35        |
| Total   | 446     | 257      | 197       |

## EUROPEAN COUNTRIES REPRESENTED (by number of players)

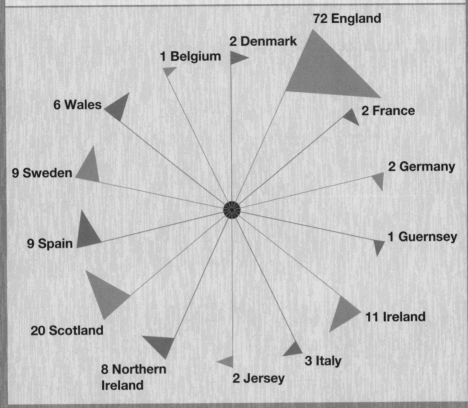

72 England

2 Denmark

1 Belgium

6 Wales

2 France

9 Sweden

2 Germany

9 Spain

1 Guernsey

20 Scotland

11 Ireland

8 Northern Ireland

3 Italy

2 Jersey

## WORST RECORDS AT RYDER CUP

| USA | WON | LOST | HALVED |
|---|---|---|---|
| Fuzzy Zoeller | 1 | 8 | 1 |
| Jerry Barber | 1 | 4 | 0 |
| Olin Dutra | 1 | 3 | 0 |
| Tommy Aaron | 1 | 4 | 1 |
| Miller Barber | 1 | 4 | 1 |
| Ben Crenshaw | 3 | 8 | 1 |

| Europe | WON | LOST | HALVED |
|---|---|---|---|
| Alf Padgham | 0 | 7 | 0 |
| Tom Haliburton | 0 | 6 | 0 |
| John Panton | 0 | 5 | 0 |
| Max Faulkner | 1 | 7 | 0 |
| Charles Ward | 1 | 5 | 0 |
| Eamonn Darcy | 1 | 8 | 2 |
| Tommy Horton | 1 | 6 | 1 |

Only 6 players in the competition's history have scored a hole-in-one:

Peter Butler 1973
Nick Faldo 1993
Costantino Rocca 1995
Howard Clark 1995
Paul Casey 2006
Scott Verplank 2006

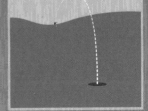

# Puck people

Number of registered ice hockey players by country

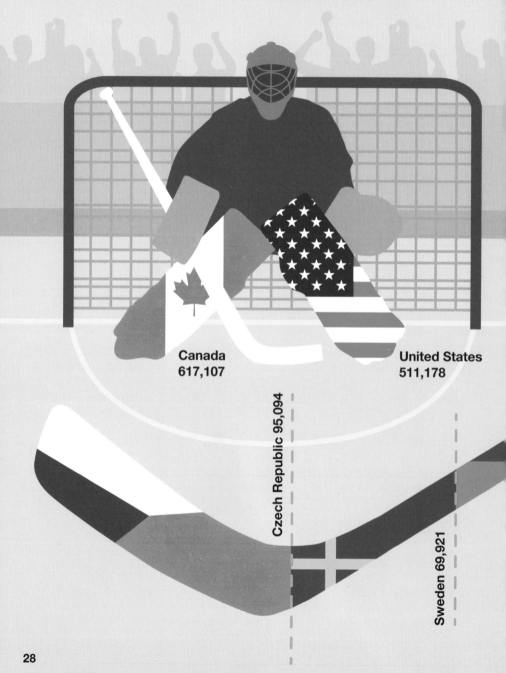

Canada
617,107

United States
511,178

Czech Republic 95,094

Sweden 69,921

Figures are from December 2012

Russia 64,326

Finland 56,626

Germany 27,068

Switzerland 26,166

Japan 19,975

France 17,381

Austria 11,202

Slovakia 9,034

# Permanent fixtures

## Old sporting rivalries that just keep going

'Old firm' derby, football

**Rangers** V **Celtic**
119 wins   100 wins
1891
304 matches (85 draws)

0000000001

Test cricket

**India** V **Pakistan**
9 wins   12 wins
1952
59 matches (38 draws)

0000000002

Ryder Cup, golf

**United States** V **Europe**
7 wins   9 wins
1979
17 matches (1 draw)

0000000003

'El Clásico', football

**Barcelona** V **Real Madrid**
64 wins   70 wins
1929
166 matches (32 draws)

0000000004

International Test Rugby

**New Zealand** V **Australia**
102 wins   41 wins
1903
149 matches (6 draws)

0000000005

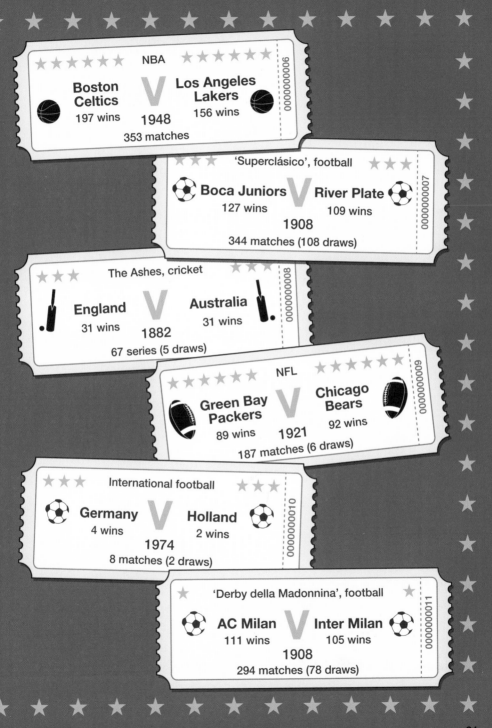

NBA

**Boston Celtics**
197 wins

V
1948

**Los Angeles Lakers**
156 wins

353 matches

0000000006

'Superclásico', football

**Boca Juniors**
127 wins

V

**River Plate**
109 wins

1908

344 matches (108 draws)

0000000007

The Ashes, cricket

**England**
31 wins

V
1882

**Australia**
31 wins

67 series (5 draws)

0000000008

NFL

**Green Bay Packers**
89 wins

V
1921

**Chicago Bears**
92 wins

187 matches (6 draws)

0000000009

International football

**Germany**
4 wins

V
1974

**Holland**
2 wins

8 matches (2 draws)

0000000010

'Derby della Madonnina', football

**AC Milan**
111 wins

V

**Inter Milan**
105 wins

1908

294 matches (78 draws)

0000000011

# Eternal flame

## Summer Olympics torch design through the decades

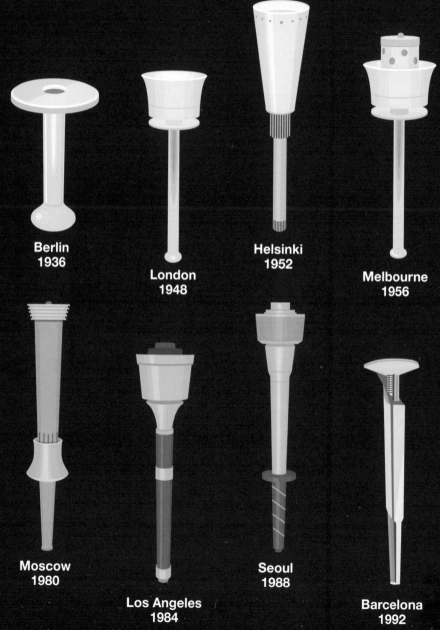

Berlin
1936

London
1948

Helsinki
1952

Melbourne
1956

Moscow
1980

Los Angeles
1984

Seoul
1988

Barcelona
1992

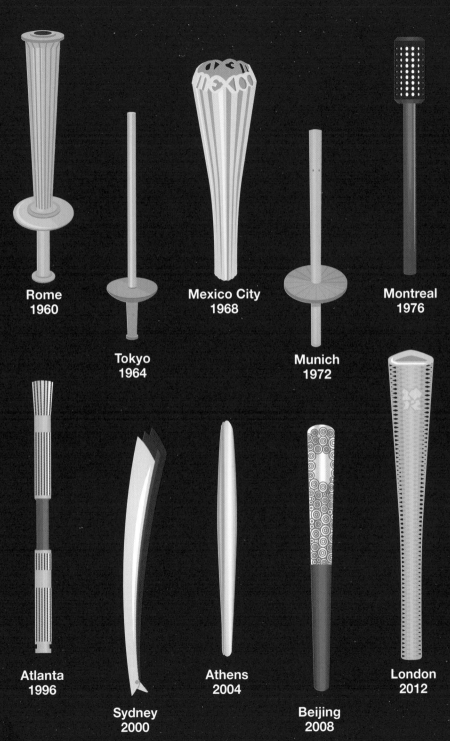

Rome
1960

Tokyo
1964

Mexico City
1968

Munich
1972

Montreal
1976

Atlanta
1996

Sydney
2000

Athens
2004

Beijing
2008

London
2012

# Sydney to Hobart

**Facts about one of the most challenging and dangerous yacht races in the world**

## 1945
Rani wins inaugural race against 8 competitors.

**AUSTRALIA**

The course is approximately 1170 km (727 miles or 630 nautical miles) long

The race starts in Sydney on Boxing Day and finishes in Hobart, Tasmania

**Since 1945**
there have been
5,509 entrants

**1994**
The most competitors
- 371 yachts started

**17.5%**
of entrants have
failed or retired

**1998**
Tragedy struck: 5 yachts
sank and 6 sailors drowned

Of 115 starters
only 43 boats
finished

**2008**
Maluka, built in 1932,
became the oldest
yacht to compete

**2012**
Fastest race time
achieved by Wild Oats
XI (NSW): 1 day,
18 hours, 23 minutes
and 12 seconds

Sydney

**BASS STRAIT**

**TASMANIA**

Hobart

# Anyone for tennis?

**The Wimbledon fortnight is not just tie-breaks and net cords**

**300,000**
cups of tea and coffee

**250,000**
bottles of water

**200,000**
glasses of Pimm's

**135,000**
ice creams

**112,000**
punnets of strawberries

**100,000**
pints of draught beer

**Price of strawberries and cream**

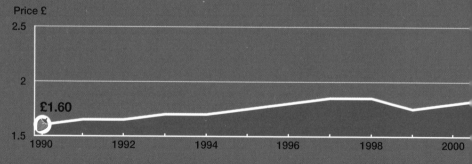

Price £

2.5

2

£1.60

1.5

1990  1992  1994  1996  1998  2000

**190,000**
sandwiches

**150,000**
Bath buns, scones,
pastries and
donuts

**150,000**
glasses of champagne

**32,000**
portions of
fish and chips

**25,000**
bottles of champagne

**23,000**
bananas

**22,000**
slices of pizza

£2.50

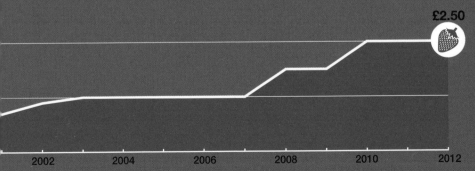

2002      2004      2006      2008      2010      2012

# Run like the wind

The fastest horses recorded at the most famous
flat races in the world

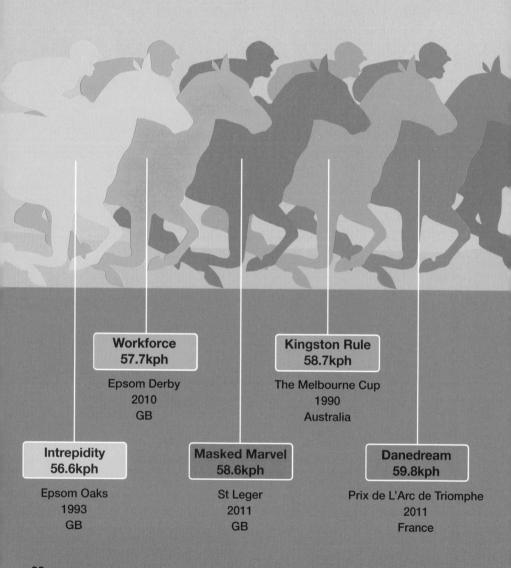

**Workforce**
**57.7kph**

Epsom Derby
2010
GB

**Kingston Rule**
**58.7kph**

The Melbourne Cup
1990
Australia

**Intrepidity**
**56.6kph**

Epsom Oaks
1993
GB

**Masked Marvel**
**58.6kph**

St Leger
2011
GB

**Danedream**
**59.8kph**

Prix de L'Arc de Triomphe
2011
France

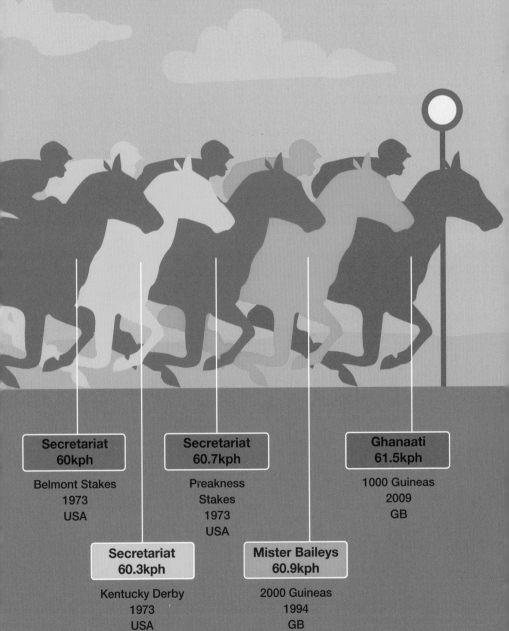

**Secretariat**
**60kph**

Belmont Stakes
1973
USA

**Secretariat**
**60.7kph**

Preakness
Stakes
1973
USA

**Ghanaati**
**61.5kph**

1000 Guineas
2009
GB

**Secretariat**
**60.3kph**

Kentucky Derby
1973
USA

**Mister Baileys**
**60.9kph**

2000 Guineas
1994
GB

# Permanent records

**Some sporting records that will (probably) never be broken**

Nearest rival
Pete Rose: 44 games in 1978

**Joe DiMaggio**
56-game hitting streak
for New York Yankees in 1941

**Geraldo Pereira de Matos Filho
('Mazarópi')**
Longest time without conceding
a goal: 1,816 minutes in 1977–8
season for CR Vasco da Gama in
Rio de Janeiro

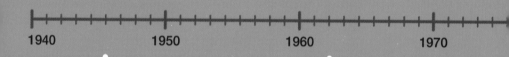

1940          1950          1960          1970

**Byron Nelson**
Won 18 of 35 PGA Tour
events in 1945, including
11 consecutive victories

**Wilt Chamberlain**
Only player to score 100 points
in an NBA game – Philadelphia
Warriors (169) v New York Knicks
in 1962

Nearest rival
Ben Hogan: 13 wins in 1946

Nearest rival:
Kobe Bryant: 81 points in 2006

Nearest rival
David Pearson: 105 wins

**Richard Petty**
200 NASCAR wins
in 1184 races, 1958–92

Nearest rival
Wayne Gretzky: 212 points (1981–2)

**Wayne Gretzky**
215 points in an NHL ice hockey
season (1985–6) and total points
in career (2,857)

1980          1990          2000          2010

**Cal Ripken Jr**
2,632 consecutive major league
baseball games for Baltimore
Orioles, 1982–98

**John Stockton**
(Utah Jazz point
guard) 15,806 assists
in 1504 NBA games,
1984–2003

Nearest rival
Lou Gehrig: 2,130 games

Nearest rival
Jason Kidd (NY Knicks)
12,012 in 1363 games

**Michael Phelps**
(swimmer) Most Olympic gold
medals won by one person
(18 – double his nearest rivals).
The most first-place finishes
at a single Olympics (8 gold
medals – Beijing 2008)

# Golden balls

The world's most expensive players ranked by the total value of their transfer fees through their careers

**ROBINHO**

**£71.74m**

Santos,
Real Madrid,
Manchester City,
AC Milan

**ZINEDINE ZIDANE**

**£70.89m**

Cannes,
Bordeaux,
Juventus,
Real Madrid

**CHRISTIAN VIERI**

**£73.85m**

Torino, Pisa, Ravenna,
Venezia, Atalanta, Juventus,
Atlético Madrid, Lazio,
Inter Milan, AC Milan,
Monaco, Sampdoria,
Fiorentina

**EDINSON CAVANI**

**£76.12m**

Danubio FC, US Palermo,
Napoli, Paris St-Germain

**FERNANDO TORRES**

**£81.44m**

Atlético Madrid,
Liverpool, Chelsea

**RONALDO**

**£85.16m**

Cruzeiro, PSV Eindhoven,
Barcelona, Inter Milan,
Real Madrid, AC Milan,
Corinthians

**ROBBIE KEANE**

**£91.38m**

Wolverhampton
Wanderers,
Coventry City,
Inter Milan, Leeds Utd,
Tottenham Hotspur,
Liverpool,
Celtic, West Ham,
LA Galaxy

**GARETH BALE**

**£92.3m**

Southampton,
Tottenham Hotspur,
Real Madrid

## ZLATAN IBRAHIMOVIĆ

### £144.41m

Malmö, Ajax, Juventus,
Inter Milan, Barcelona,
AC Milan,
Paris St-Germain

## NICOLAS ANELKA

### £113.09m

Paris St-Germain, Arsenal,
Real Madrid, Liverpool,
Manchester City, Fenerbahçe,
Bolton Wanderers, Chelsea,
Shanghai Shenhua, Juventus,
West Brom

## HERNÁN CRESPO

### £102.12m

River Plate, Parma, Lazio,
Inter Milan, Chelsea, Genoa,
Barasat Euro Musketeers

## FALCAO

### £98.86m

River Plate, FC Porto,
Atlético Madrid,
AS Monaco

## JUAN VERÓN

### £98.75m

Estudiantes, Boca Juniors,
Sampdoria, Parma,
Lazio, Manchester Utd,
Chelsea

## CRISTIANO RONALDO

### £94.1m

Sporting CP,
Manchester Utd,
Real Madrid

# Tic-tac

## The secret language of bookies

**9–4 (nut)**
Both hands on top of the head

**7–4 (neves to rouf)**
Right hand on shoulder

**2–1 (bottle/bice)**
Right hand touches nose

**7–2 (carpet and a half)**
Both hands touch chest

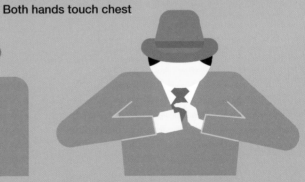

**3–1(carpet)**
Hand to chin, palm facing down

**10–1 (cockle)**
Fists together, right thumb upwards
(like a 10)

45

# On your marks

**The world athletics records that have lasted the longest**

## Men

Jürgen Schult 1386 weeks
Discus
1986 74.08m

Yuriy Sedykh 1374 weeks
Hammer throw
1986 86.74m

Randy Barnes 1180weeks
Shot put
1990 23.12m

Mike Powell 1113 weeks
Long jump
1991 8.95m

Kevin Young 1064 weeks
400m hurdles
1992 46.78 seconds

Javier Sotomayor 1014 weeks
High jump
1993 2.45m

Sergey Bubka 961 weeks
Pole vault
1994 6.14m

Jonathan Edwards 908 weeks
Triple jump
1995 18.29m

Jan Železný 866 weeks
Javelin
1996 98.48m

Hicham El Guerrouj 755 weeks
1500m
1998 3:26:00

Michael Johnson 696 weeks
400m
1999 43.18 seconds

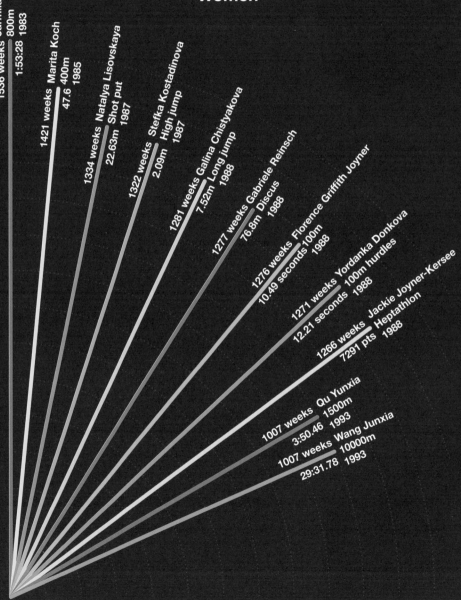

Women

1536 weeks Jarmila Kratochvílová
800m
1:53:28 1983

1421 weeks Marita Koch
400m
47.6 1985

1334 weeks Natalya Lisovskaya
Shot put
22.63m 1987

1322 weeks Stefka Kostadinova
High jump
2.09m 1987

1281 weeks Galina Chistyakova
Long jump
7.52m 1988

1277 weeks Gabriele Reinsch
Discus
76.8m 1988

1276 weeks Florence Griffith Joyner
100m
10.49 seconds 1988

1271 weeks Yordanka Donkova
100m hurdles
12.21 seconds 1988

1266 weeks Jackie Joyner-Kersee
Heptathlon
7291 pts 1988

1007 weeks Qu Yunxia
1500m
3:50.46 1993

1007 weeks Wang Junxia
10000m
29:31.78 1993

# Moving the goalposts

## The relative size of goals in different sports

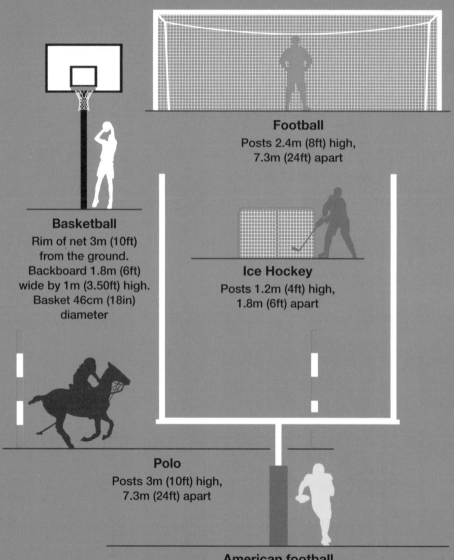

**Football**
Posts 2.4m (8ft) high,
7.3m (24ft) apart

**Basketball**
Rim of net 3m (10ft)
from the ground.
Backboard 1.8m (6ft)
wide by 1m (3.50ft) high.
Basket 46cm (18in)
diameter

**Ice Hockey**
Posts 1.2m (4ft) high,
1.8m (6ft) apart

**Polo**
Posts 3m (10ft) high,
7.3m (24ft) apart

**American football**
Posts 3m (10ft) high minimum, 9.1m (30ft) high shown.
Posts 5.6m (18.50ft) apart. Crossbar 3m (10ft) from the ground

**Cricket**
Stumps 0.7m (28in) high,
22.8cm (9in) wide

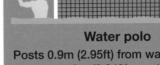

**Water polo**
Posts 0.9m (2.95ft) from water surface,
3m (9.84ft) apart.

**Hockey**
Posts 2.1m (6.88ft) high,
3.6m (11.81ft) apart.

**Lacrosse**
Posts 1.8m (6ft) high,
Posts 1.8m (6ft) apart

**Rugby Union & Rugby League**
Posts 3.4m (11.15ft) high minimum, 16m high (52.49ft) shown.
Posts 5.5m (18.05ft) apart. Crossbar 3m (9.84ft) from the ground

# Breaking records

World records from the United States
and World Breaking Association

## 6 coconuts
### broken in 10 seconds

Ralph Bergamo
Orlando, FL
2012

## 33 steel bars
### bent with the throat
### in 30 seconds

Fernando Camareno
Puerto Rico
2005

## 13 baseball bats
### broken with an elbow
### in 10 seconds

Larry Fields
Orlando, FL
2011

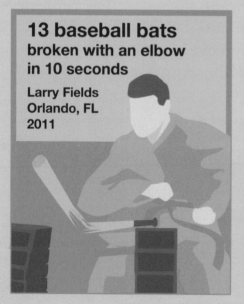

## 5 wooden planks
### broken with a kick
### in 10 seconds

John Zurisk
Michigan City, IN
2011

## 468 concrete tiles
### broken in 60 seconds

**Fernando Camareno**
**Puerto Rico**
**2007**

## 113 concrete blocks
### broken with an elbow in 10 seconds

**Larry Fields**
**Uncasville, CT**
**2008**

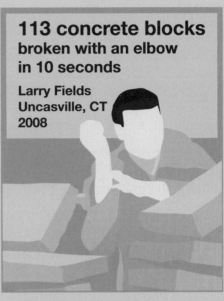

## 126 boards
### broken in 10 seconds

**Gary Reho**
**Fairfield, CT**
**2009**

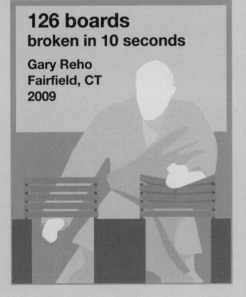

## 236 concrete blocks
### broken with a stomp

**Nick Zambri**
**Orlando, FL**
**2013**

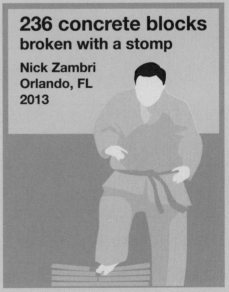

Source: The United States and World Breaking Association (http://usbawba.org/)

# How fast can he go?

## Men's 100m Olympic gold medallists since 1896

| | | 12.0 | 11.5 |
|---|---|---|---|
| 1896 | Thomas Burke (USA) 12.0 | | |
| 1900 | Francis Jarvis (USA) 11.0 | | |
| 1904 | Archie Hahn (USA) 11.0 | | |
| 1908 | Reginald Walker (RSA) 10.8 | | |
| 1912 | Ralph Craig (USA) 10.8 | | |
| 1920 | Charley Paddock (USA) 10.8 | | |
| 1924 | Harold Abrahams (GBR) 10.6 | | |
| 1928 | Percy Williams (CAN) 10.8 | | |
| 1932 | Eddie Tolan (USA) 10.3 | | |
| 1936 | Jesse Owens (USA) 10.3 | | |
| 1948 | Harrison Dillard (USA) 10.3 | | |
| 1952 | Lindy Remigino (USA) 10.4 | | |
| 1956 | Bobby Morrow (USA) 10.5 | | |
| 1960 | Armin Hary (GER) 10.2 | | |
| 1964 | Bob Hayes (USA) 10.0 | | |
| 1968 | Jim Hines (USA) 9.95 | | |
| 1972 | Valery Borzov (URS) 10.14 | | |
| 1972 | Hasely Crawford (TRI) 10.06 | | |
| 1980 | Allan Wells (GBR) 10.25 | | |
| 1984 | Carl Lewis (USA) 9.99 | | |
| 1988 | Carl Lewis (USA) 9.92 | | |
| 1992 | Linford Christie (GBR) 9.96 | | |
| 1996 | Donovan Bailey (CAN) 9.84 | | |
| 2000 | Maurice Greene (USA) 9.87 | | |
| 2004 | Justin Gatlin (USA) 9.85 | | |
| 2008 | Usain Bolt (JAM) 9.69 | | |
| 2012 | Usain Bolt (JAM) 9.63 | | |

**11.0**     **10.5**     **10.0**     **9.6**

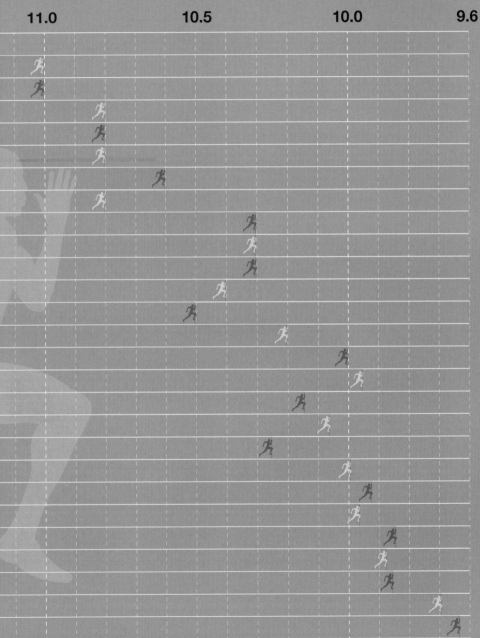

# How fast can she go?

**Women's Olympic 100m gold medallists since 1928**

|      |                                        | 12.0 |
|------|----------------------------------------|------|
| 1928 | Elizabeth Robinson (USA) 12.2          |      |
| 1932 | Stanislawa Walasiewicz (POL) 11.9      |      |
| 1936 | Helen Stephens (USA) 11.5              |      |
| 1948 | Fanny Blankers-Koen (NED) 11.9         |      |
| 1952 | Marjorie Jackson (AUS) 11.5            |      |
| 1956 | Betty Cuthbert (AUS) 11.5              |      |
| 1960 | Wilma Rudolph (USA) 11.0               |      |
| 1964 | Wyomia Tyus (USA) 11.4                 |      |
| 1968 | Wyomia Tyus (USA) 11.0                 |      |
| 1972 | Renate Stecher (GDR) 11.07             |      |
| 1976 | Annegret Richter (FRG) 11.08           |      |
| 1980 | Lyudmila Kondratyeva (URS) 11.06       |      |
| 1984 | Evelyn Ashford (USA) 10.97             |      |
| 1988 | Florence Griffith Joyner (USA) 10.54   |      |
| 1992 | Gail Devers (USA) 10.82                |      |
| 1996 | Gail Devers (USA) 10.94                |      |
| 2000 | Ekaterini Thanou (GRE) 11.12           |      |
| 2004 | Yuliya Nesterenko (BLR) 10.93          |      |
| 2008 | Shelly-Ann Fraser-Pryce (JAM) 10.78    |      |
| 2012 | Shelly-Ann Fraser-Pryce (JAM) 10.75    |      |

Seconds to complete 100m

# Oarsome

**Greatest margins of victory in the Oxford v Cambridge Varsity Boat Race measured in boat lengths**

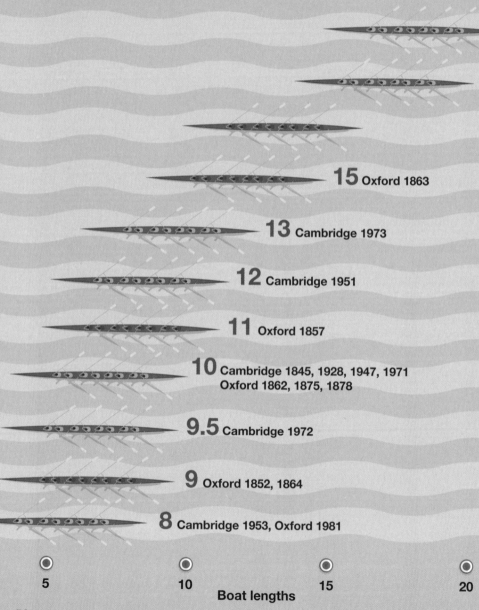

**15** Oxford 1863

**13** Cambridge 1973

**12** Cambridge 1951

**11** Oxford 1857

**10** Cambridge 1845, 1928, 1947, 1971
Oxford 1862, 1875, 1878

**9.5** Cambridge 1972

**9** Oxford 1852, 1864

**8** Cambridge 1953, Oxford 1981

5          10          15          20

**Boat lengths**

**35** Cambridge 1839

**22** Cambridge 1841

**20** Cambridge 1836, 1900

**16** Oxford 1861, Cambridge 1955

The course is 4 miles 374 yards (6.8km) between Putney and Mortlake on the River Thames in London

The only dead heat took place in 1877

In 1912 both crews sank, a few weeks before the *Titanic*

2003 saw the smallest margin of victory when Oxford won by a foot

Longest winning streak: 1924–36 (13 wins, Cambridge)

25          30          35

# Paralympic greats

**Paralympians with over 20 medals ranked by number of golds**

## 2. Ragnhild Myklebust
Norway
1988–2002

22
3
2

Nordic skiing

## 1. Trischa Zorn
USA
1980–2004

41
9
5

Swimming

## 4. Béatrice Hess
France
1984–2004

18
5

Swimming

## 3. Reinhild Möller
Germany
1980–2006

19
3
1

Skiing

## 5. Jonas Jacobsson
Sweden
1980–2012

17
4
9

Shooting

## 6. Mike Kenny
Great Britain
1976–88

16
2

Swimming

## 7-9. Roberto Marson
Italy
1964–76

16
7
3

Athletics, Swimming, Fencing

## 10. Gerd Schönfelder

Germany
1992–2010

16
4
2

Skiing

## 11-13. Heinz Frei

Switzerland
1982–2000

16
6
11

Athletics, Cycling, Nordic skiing

## 14. Mayumi Narita

Japan
1996–2004

15
3
2

Swimming

## 15. Chantal Petitclerc

Canada
1992–2008

14
5
2

Athletics

## 16. Franz Nietlispach

Switzerland
1980–2000

14
6
2

Athletics

## 17-19. Frank Höfle

Germany
1992–2002

14
5
5

Biathlon, Cross-country
skiing, Cycling

# Messi magic

How Lionel Messi scored a record-breaking 91 goals, for Barcelona and Argentina, during 2012

**3**
Head

**8**
Right foot

**80**
Left foot

# 13

**Outside the penalty box**

# 78

**Inside the penalty box**

- 6 hat-tricks
- 1st, 2nd, 10th, 14th, 15th, 46th and 69th minutes of matches were the only ones Messi didn't score in during 2012 calendar year
- His longest 'goal drought' was three games
- Scored 12 goals for Argentina – equalling Gabriel Batistuta's record in a season
- 8 Champions League goals

# Size matters

## The relative size of balls used in sport

**SOCCER**
226mm

**BASKETBALL**
239mm

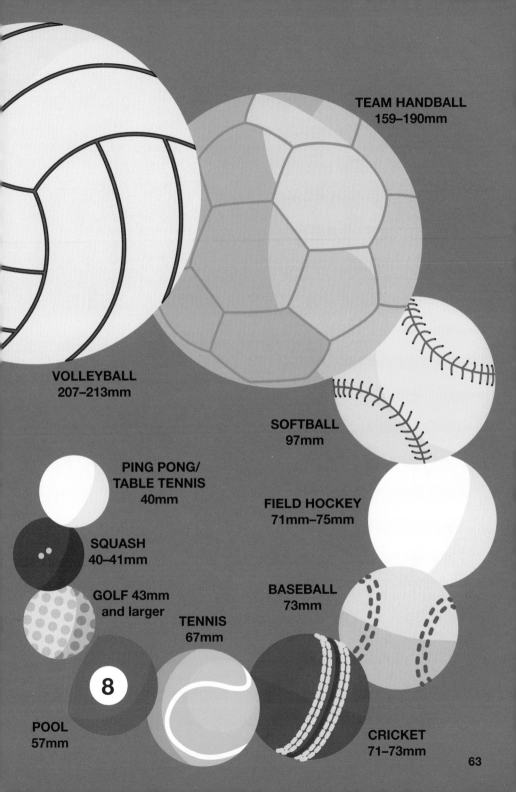

TEAM HANDBALL
159–190mm

VOLLEYBALL
207–213mm

SOFTBALL
97mm

PING PONG/
TABLE TENNIS
40mm

FIELD HOCKEY
71mm–75mm

SQUASH
40–41mm

GOLF 43mm
and larger

BASEBALL
73mm

TENNIS
67mm

8

POOL
57mm

CRICKET
71–73mm

63

# Sweeping on ice

## How does curling work?

 A team scores a point for each stone placed closer to the centre of the house than their opponents' best stone

 One game consists of up to 10 'ends'. During each end, each team of four delivers eight stones – two stones per person

 Curling was one of the sports in the first Winter Olympic Games at Chamonix in 1924. Great Britain won the first gold medal

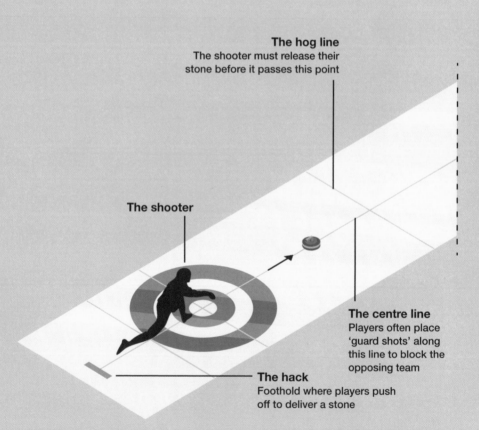

**The hog line**
The shooter must release their stone before it passes this point

**The shooter**

**The centre line**
Players often place 'guard shots' along this line to block the opposing team

**The hack**
Foothold where players push off to deliver a stone

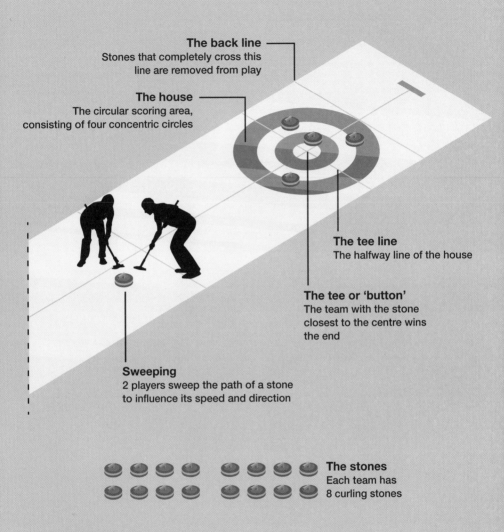

**The back line**
Stones that completely cross this line are removed from play

**The house**
The circular scoring area, consisting of four concentric circles

**The tee line**
The halfway line of the house

**The tee or 'button'**
The team with the stone closest to the centre wins the end

**Sweeping**
2 players sweep the path of a stone to influence its speed and direction

**The stones**
Each team has 8 curling stones

## The curling sheet

Width: 5m / 16.4ft

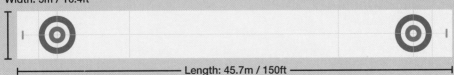

Length: 45.7m / 150ft

# Blink and you miss it

## Fastest knock-outs in boxing world title fights

Daniel Jiménez
Harold Geier (KO)
Super-Bantamweight
1994

Gerald McClellan
Jay Bell (KO)
Middleweight
1993

Shannon Briggs
John Sargent (KO)
Heavyweight
2003

Chris Eubank
Reginaldo Dos Santos (KO)
Middleweight
1990

Pongsaklek Wonjongkam
Daisuke Naito (KO)
Flyweight
2002

Mike Tyson
Michael Spinks (KO)
Heavyweight
1988

Bernard Hopkins
Steve Frank (KO)
Middleweight
1996

Prince Naseem Hamed
Said Lawal (KO)
Featherweight
1996

# Tracking shoes

## A timeline of the running shoe

### 1830s
First rubber soled canvas shoe developed as beachwear by the Liverpool Rubber Company

### 1899
First patent for rubber heel for shoes awarded to Humphrey O'Sullivan

### 1925
German Adolf 'Adi' Dassler creates hand-forged spikes – different spikes for different distances. He and his brother Rudo run the Dassler Brothers Shoe Factory

### 1936
US runner Jesse Owens wins four gold medals at Berlin Olympics wearing Adolf Dassler's 'spikes'

### 1970s
Podiatrists define three types of running style:

#### 1. NEUTRAL
Foot travels in a straight line as it moves forward

#### 2. PRONATION
Ankle moves to the inside

#### 3. SUPINATION
Ankle moves to the outside

### 1948
After Rudolf leaves to form new firm Puma, Adolf Dassler renames the company 'Adidas'

1  2  3

## 1890
J.W. Foster invents
'spiked' running shoe in UK

## 1895
J.W. Foster & Sons
set up shop
(renamed Reebok in 1958)

## 1907
Spalding company
introduces first
basketball shoe

## 1917
Keds shoe company set
up to sell sneakers to USA

The term 'sneaker' coined
by an advertising agency –
because you could
sneak around on the
quiet rubber soles

## 1979
Nike Air incorporates air
bubble in heel of Tailwind
running shoe for cushioning.
Widely copied

## 2013
Around 350 million pairs
of sports shoes are purchased
each year in the USA

# Different strokes

The most common paddle strokes used to propel and manoeuvre canoes and kayaks

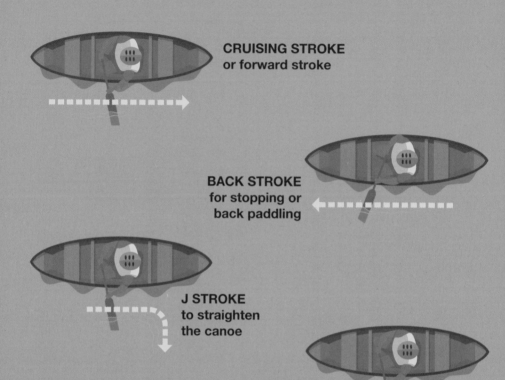

**CRUISING STROKE**
or forward stroke

**BACK STROKE**
for stopping or
back paddling

**J STROKE**
to straighten
the canoe

**CANADIAN J STROKE**
for going straight against
strong wind or currents

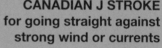

**PRY STROKE**
to move canoe in opposite
direction from the paddling side

**DRAW STROKE**
opposite effect to
pry stroke

**SCULL**
paddler's end of canoe
drawn to paddling side

**REVERSE SCULL**
paddler's end of canoe pushed
away from paddling side

**SWEEP**
steers canoe
away from paddle

**C-STROKE**
used in solo canoeing
to turn canoe to the side
opposite of paddler

# Bullseye

## Darts facts by numbers

The year Welshman Leighton Rees won the first darts World Championship — **1978**

There are 2 leading darts organisations – the BDO* and the PDC** — **2**

The record number of times Englishman Phil Taylor has won the World Championship — **16**

The maximum weight of a dart is 50g — **50**

The maximum length of a dart is 30.5cm (12in) — **30.5**

The average speed of a flying dart is 64kph (40mph) — **64**

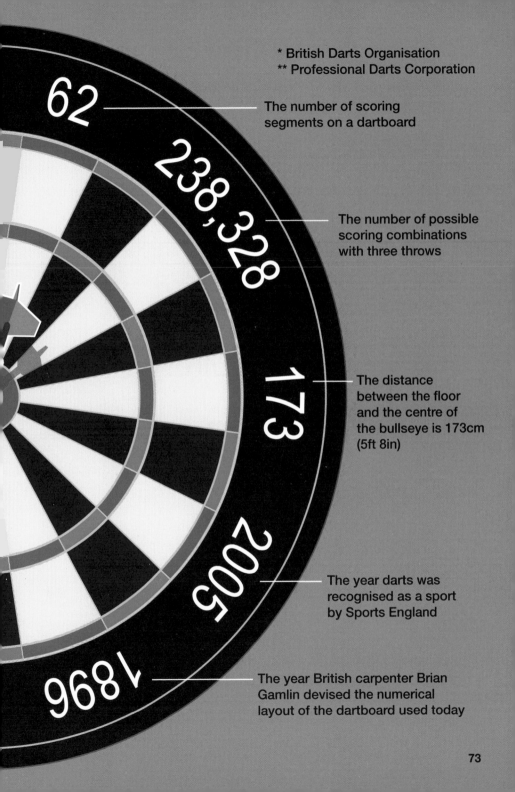

* British Darts Organisation
** Professional Darts Corporation

**62** — The number of scoring segments on a dartboard

**238,328** — The number of possible scoring combinations with three throws

**173** — The distance between the floor and the centre of the bullseye is 173cm (5ft 8in)

**2005** — The year darts was recognised as a sport by Sports England

**1896** — The year British carpenter Brian Gamlin devised the numerical layout of the dartboard used today

# Calorie-controlled

**Least and most calories burned in one hour in different sports and activities**

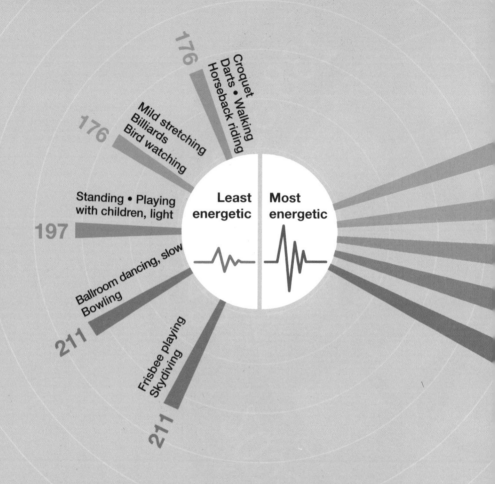

176 — Croquet • Darts • Walking • Horseback riding

176 — Mild stretching • Billiards • Bird watching

197 — Standing • Playing with children, light

211 — Ballroom dancing, slow • Bowling

211 — Frisbee playing • Skydiving

Least energetic

Most energetic

Calories calculated for a male weighing 70kg (155lb)

Cycling, very fast, 17.5mph/28kph
Squash • Handball • Jumping rope, fast    844

Skin diving, moderate    880

Cross-country skiing, racing    985

Running up stairs • Competitive speed skating    1056

Cycling, racing >20mph/32kph • Running, 10mph/16kph    1126

# On course

## Strange facts from the world of professional golf

The world's longest golf course is Nullabor Links, Australia. The 18-hole, par 72 course spans nearly 1,368 kilometres (850 miles), with as much as 80 kilometres (50 miles) between holes

The driver swing speed of an average lady golfer is 62mph (100kph); 84mph (135kph) for an average male golfer; 108mph (174kph) for an average PGA Tour player, while Tiger Woods' average driver swing speed is 130mph (209kph)

125,000 golf balls a year are hit into the water at the famous 17th hole of the Stadium Course at Sawgrass in Florida

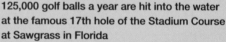

A golf course within 4 miles (6.5 km) of the coast is called a links

The longest drive ever recorded is 515 yards (471 metres), hit by 64-year-old Mike Austin in the 1974 US National Seniors Open in Las Vegas (now known as 'Desert Rose')

The oldest player to score his age is C. Arthur Thompson (1869–1975) of Victoria, British Columbia, Canada, who scored 103 on the Uplands Course of 6,215 yards (5683 metres), aged 103 in 1973

The highest golf course in the world is the Tactu Golf Club in Morococha, Peru, which sits 4,369 metres (14,335 feet) above sea level at its lowest point

300 million golf balls are lost or discarded in the US each year

Americans spend more than $630 million a year on golf balls

The longest recorded putt is 375 feet (114.3 metres) by 66-year-old Fergus Muir at the 5th hole at St Andrew's Eden Course in 2001

There are 336 dimples on a typical regulation golf ball

It can take between 100 and 1,000 years for a golf ball to decompose

# Funding the Olympians

The cost per medal for Team GB at the London 2012
Olympic Games

**SWIMMING**
Cost per medal:
£8,381,533

**DIVING**
Cost per medal:
£6,535,700

**MODERN PENTATHLON**
Cost per medal:
£6,288,800

**SAILING**
Cost per medal:
£4,588,540

**ATHLETICS**
Cost per medal:
£4,191,333

**CANOEING**
Cost per medal:
£4,044,175

**JUDO**
Cost per medal:
£3,749,000

**ROWING**
Cost per medal:
£3,031,956

**GYMNASTICS**
Cost per medal:
£2,692,650

**EQUESTRIAN**
Cost per medal:
£2,679,020

**TRIATHLON**
Cost per medal:
£2,645,650

**SHOOTING**
Cost per medal:
£2,461,866

**TAEKWONDO**
Cost per medal:
£2,416,800

**CYCLING**
Cost per medal:
£2,169,333

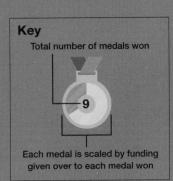

**Key**
Total number of medals won
9
Each medal is scaled by funding
given over to each medal won

# Funding the Paralympians

The cost per medal for Team GB at the London 2012
Paralympic Games

**ADAPTIVE ROWING**
Cost per medal:
£2,332,300

**BOCCIA**
Cost per medal:
£1,166,650

**POWERLIFTING**
Cost per medal:
£1,092,700

**DISABILITY ARCHERY**
Cost per medal:
£1,073,850

**DISABILITY SAILING**
Cost per medal:
£874,450

**DISABILITY
SHOOTING**
Cost per medal:
£695,000

**JUDO
(VISUALLY IMPAIRED)**
Cost per medal:
£647,200

**DISABILITY TABLE
TENNIS**
Cost per medal:
£424,850

**WHEELCHAIR
TENNIS**
Cost per medal:
£404,800

**PARA-EQUESTRIAN DRESSAGE**
Cost per medal:
£327,773

**DISABILITY SWIMMING**
Cost per medal: £268,429

**DISABILITY ATHLETICS**
Cost per medal:
£232,069

**PARA-CYCLING**
Cost per medal:
£190,818

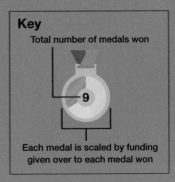

**Key**

Total number of medals won

9

Each medal is scaled by funding
given over to each medal won

# Major league success

## Most successful teams, ranked by percentage of championships won in their league

**MONTREAL CANADIENS**
NHL Stanley Cup
Finals winners
(Ice hockey)
Title wins: 24
Seasons: 97

**BOSTON CELTICS**
NBA
Title wins: 17
Seasons: 67

**SANTOS & PAMEIRAS**
Campeonato Brasileiro
Série A
(Brazilian football)
Title wins: 8 each
Seasons: 56

**NEW YORK YANKEES**
Major League Baseball
World Series winners
Title wins: 27
Seasons: 108

**REAL MADRID**
Euroleague basketball
Titles won: 8
Seasons: 56

| 14.3% | 14.3% | 24.5% | 25% | 25.5% |

Percentage of seasons played in which the team won the title

**YOMIURI GIANTS**
Japan Championship
Series (Baseball)
Title wins: 22
Seasons: 63

**REAL MADRID**
La Liga
(Spanish football)
Title wins: 32
Seasons: 82

**RIVER PLATE**
Primera División
(Argentine football)
Title wins: 34
Seasons: 83

**AFC AJAX**
Eredivisie
(Dutch football)
Title wins: 24
Seasons: 57

**BAYERN MUNICH**
Bundesliga
(German football)
Title wins: 22
Seasons: 50

**MANCHESTER UNITED**
Premier League
Title wins: 13
Seasons: 21

34.9%     39%     41%     42%     44%     62%

Percentage of seasons played in which the team won the title

**Martina Navratilova**
TENNIS
49 Grand Slam titles

**Rod Laver**
TENNIS
11 Grand Slam titles

**Phil Mickelson**
GOLF
4 majors and 40 PGA
tour championships

**Manny Pacquiao**
BOXING
10 titles across 8 weight
divisions

\* OPS (On-base Plus Slugging) and OPS+ (On-base Plus Slugging Plus) are statistical measures of a batter's power and effectiveness at getting on-base.

**Brian Lara**
CRICKET
11,952 Test runs and the only player to have scored a quadruple hundred in a Test match

**Babe Ruth**
BASEBALL
1st all-time slugging percentage
1st all-time OPS*
1st all-time OPS+*

**Wasim Akram**
CRICKET
Second on all-time list of One Day International bowlers with a strike rate of 36.2

**Lin Dan**
BADMINTON
Winner of every possible world championship and medal

# Big League collecting

## Ten of the most valuable baseball cards of all time

**Honus Wagner**
1909 White Borders
(Piedmont & Sweet Caporal)
**$2,800,000**

**Babe Ruth**
1914 Baltimore News
**$517,000**

**Roberto Clemente**
1955 Topps
**$432,690**

**Joe Doyle**
1909 White Borders
(Piedmont & Sweet Caporal)
**$329,000**

**Mickey Mantle**
1952 Topps
**$282,000**

**6**

**7**

### Lou Gehrig
1933 Goudey
**$275,000**

### Ty Cobb
1911 General Baking Co.
**$273,000**

**8**

**10**

**9**

### Honus Wagner
1910 Standard Caramel
**$219,000**

### Eddie Plank
1909 White Borders
(Piedmont & Sweet Caporal)
**$194,000**

### Joe Jackson
1914 Boston Garter
**$204,000**

# It was *this* big

**Largest verified catches of different kinds of freshwater fish**

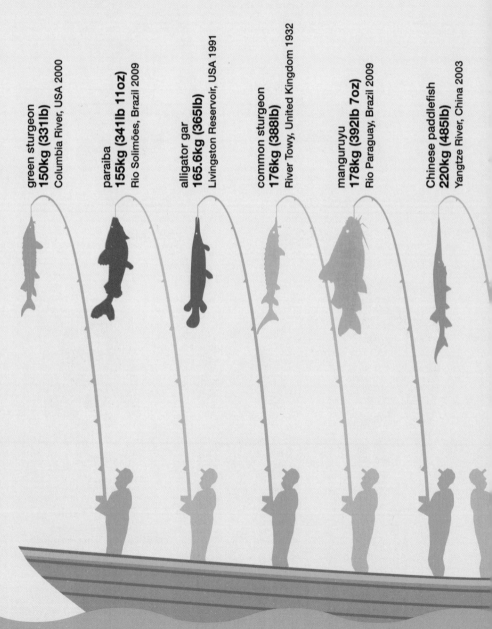

green sturgeon
**150kg (331lb)**
Columbia River, USA 2000

paraiba
**155kg (341lb 11oz)**
Rio Solimões, Brazil 2009

alligator gar
**165.6kg (365lb)**
Livingston Reservoir, USA 1991

common sturgeon
**176kg (388lb)**
River Towy, United Kingdom 1932

manguruyu
**178kg (392lb 7oz)**
Rio Paraguay, Brazil 2009

Chinese paddlefish
**220kg (485lb)**
Yangtze River, China 2003

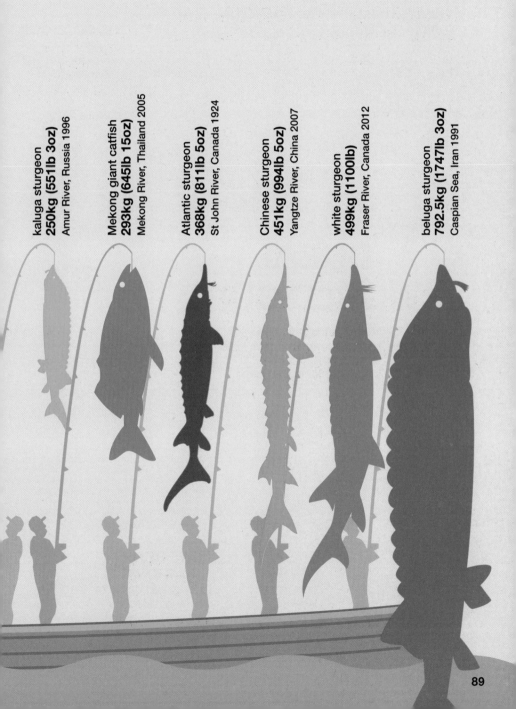

kaluga sturgeon
**250kg (551lb 3oz)**
Amur River, Russia 1996

Mekong giant catfish
**293kg (645lb 15oz)**
Mekong River, Thailand 2005

Atlantic sturgeon
**368kg (811lb 5oz)**
St John River, Canada 1924

Chinese sturgeon
**451kg (994lb 5oz)**
Yangtze River, China 2007

white sturgeon
**499kg (1100lb)**
Fraser River, Canada 2012

beluga sturgeon
**792.5kg (1747lb 3oz)**
Caspian Sea, Iran 1991

# Courses for horses

The world's most famous horse races and
the total prize money (purse) per race

## THE GOLD CUP
£350,000 ($567,420)
Royal Ascot, UK; 1807
2.5 miles (4km)
1st £198,485 ($322,000)

## DUBAI WORLD CUP

$10,000,000 (£6,250,000)
Dubai, United Arab Emirates; 1996
1.25 miles (2km)
1st $6,000,000 (£3,750,000)

## THE GRAND NATIONAL
£975,000 ($1,581,000)
Aintree, UK; 1839
4.5 miles (7.25km)
1st £547,000 ($887,000)

**KENTUCKY DERBY**
$2,000,000 (£1,250,000)
Kentucky, USA; 1875
First leg of the
US Triple Crown
1.25 miles (2km)
1st $1,425,000
(£890,000)

# US TRIPLE CROWN

**THE PREAKNESS STAKES**
$1,000,000 (£617,000)
Baltimore, USA; 1873
Second leg of the
US Triple Crown
1.2 miles (1.9 km)
1st $600,000 (£370,000)

**BELMONT STAKES**
$1,000,000
(£617,000)
New York, USA; 1867
Final leg of the US Triple Crown
1.5 miles (2.4 km)
1st $600,000 (£370,000)

**PRIX DE L'ARC DE TRIOMPHE**
€4,000,000 (£3,375,000)
Paris, France; 1920
1.5 miles (2.4km)
1st €2,285,600
(£1,929,000)

# MELBOURNE CUP

AU$6,175,000
(£3,607,000)
Melbourne, Australia; 1861
2 miles (3.2km)
1st AU$3,300,000
(£1,927,545)

# Going the distance

## Olympic marathon gold winners

London Stephen Kiprotich 02:08:01

London Tiki Gelana 02:18:58

Beijing Samuel Wanjiru 02:06:32

Beijing Constantina Tomescu 02:26:44

Athens Stefano Baldini 02:10:55

Athens Mizuki Noguchi 02:26:20

Sydney Gezahegne Abera 02:10:11

Sydney Naoko Takahashi 02:23:14

Atlanta Josia Thugwane 02:12:36

Atlanta Fatuma Roba 02:26:05

Barcelona Hwang Young-cho 02:13:23

Barcelona Valentina Yegorova 02:32:41

Seoul Gelindo Bordin 02:10:32

Seoul Rosa Mota 02:25:40

Los Angeles Carlos Lopes 02:09:21

Los Angeles Joan Benoit 02:24:52

Moscow Waldemar Cierpinski 02:11:03

Montreal Waldemar Cierpinski 02:09:55

Munich Frank Shorter 02:12:19

Mexico City Mamo Wolde 02:20:26

Tokyo Abebe Bikila 02:12:11

2012 2012 2008 2008 2004 2004 2000 2000 1996 1996 1992 1992 1988 1988 1984 1984 1980 1976 1972 1968 1964

1896 Athens Spyridon Louis 02:58:50
1900 Paris Michel Théato 02:59:45
1904 St Louis Thomas Hicks 03:28:53
1908 London Johnny Hayes 02:55:18
1912 Stockholm Ken McArthur 02:36:55
1920 Antwerp Hannes Kolehmainen 02:32:36
1924 Paris Albin Stenroos 02:41:22
1928 Amsterdam Boughèra El Ouafi 02:32:57
1932 Los Angeles Juan Carlos Zabala 02:29:19
1936 Berlin Sohn Kee-Chung 02:29:19
1948 London Delfo Cabrera 02:34:51
1952 Helsinki Emil Zátopek 02:23:03
1956 Melbourne Alain Mimoun 02:25:00
1960 Rome Abebe Bikila 02:15:16

# 4-4-GOAL

## The most successful football formations at the World Cup

**Uruguay 1930**
**Italy 1934**
**Italy 1938**
### 2-3-5

**Uruguay 1950**
**Brazil 1962**
### 4-3-3

**Germany 1954**
### 3-2-2-3

**Brazil 1958, 1970**
**West Germany 1974**
**Argentina 1978**
### 4-2-4

**England 1966**
**Brazil 1994**
### 4-4-2

**Italy 1982**
### 5-2-3

### Argentina 1986
## 3-5-2

### West Germany 1990
## 5-3-2

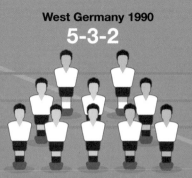

### France 1998
## 4-3-2-1

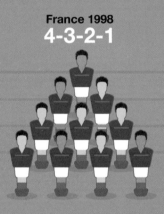

### Brazil 2002
## 3-4-3

### Italy 2006
## 4-4-1-1

### Spain 2010
## 4-2-3-1

# Might as well jump

## Some facts about Olympic ski jumping

Norwegian Ole Rye was the first recognised ski jumper, reaching 9.5m in 1808

Ski jumping featured in the first Olympic Winter Games in Chamonix Mont-Blanc in 1924

### Top ski jumping Olympic medallists

| Matti Nykänen | Simon Ammann | Jens Weissflog |
|---|---|---|
| Finland | Switzerland | Germany |
| Calgary 1988 | Vancouver 2010 | Lillehammer 1994 |
| 3 gold | 2 gold | 2 gold |
| Sarajevo 1984 | Salt Lake City 2002 | Sarajevo 1984 |
| 1 gold, 1 silver | 2 gold | 1 gold, 1 silver |

The binding must be mounted parallel to the run-direction. The binding must be placed in such a way that maximum 57% of the entire ski length is used as the front part

Skis with a maximum length of 146% of the total body height of the competitor can be used

Take-off: jumper leaves ramp at high speed (up to 60mph/97kph)

In-flight: positioning skis in a V-shape increases length of jump

Each ski jump hill has a 'K point', which is the par distance. Jumpers must aim to land beyond this to score highly

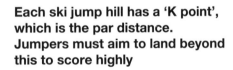

Landing: telemark position – knees bent, and one ski further forward than the other

Points are awarded for distance and style

The world record for longest ski jump is held by Norwegian Johan Remen Evensen: 246.5m in 2011

# Raising the roof

Some of the world's most iconic sporting stadia

Name: Estádio do Maracanã

Hosts: Brazil National Stadium

Built: 1950 (renovated 2013)

Capacity: 78,000

Name: Stadium Australia

Hosts: Sydney Olympics 2000

Built: 1999

Capacity: 83,500

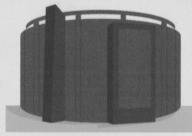

Name: Madison Square Garden

Hosts: New York Knicks (basketball)
       New York Rangers (NHL)

Built: 1968

Capacity: 19,000

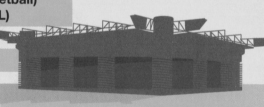

Name: San Siro

Hosts: AC Milan; Inter Milan

Built: 1926

Capacity: 80,000

**Name: Soldier Field**

**Hosts: Chicago Bears (NFL)**

**Built: 1924 (renovated 2003)**

**Capacity: 61,500**

**Name: Yankee Stadium**

**Hosts: New York Yankees (baseball)**

**Built: 2009**

**Capacity: 50,000**

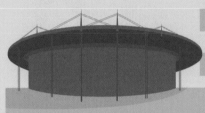

**Name: Stade de France**

**Hosts: French national football
and rugby union teams**

**Built: 1998**

**Capacity: 80,000**

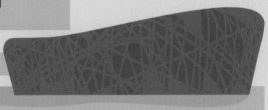

**Name: Beijing National Stadium**

**Hosts: Beijing Olympics & Paralympics**

**Built: 2008**

**Capacity: 80,000**

**Name: Wembley Stadium**

**Hosts: England national football team**

**Built: 2007**

**Capacity: 90,000**

# Float like a butterfly

Boxing punches and defences

Hook

Cross

Jab

PUNCHES

Uppercut

Overhand
(overcut)

Slipping

Blocking

DEFENCES

Pulling away

Bobbing

Cover-up
(using
gloves)

# Give me a ring

## Recent changes to the listed events at the Olympic Games

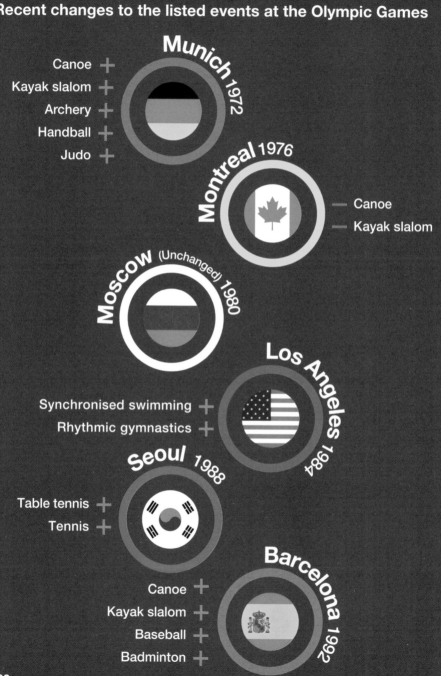

**Munich** 1972
- Canoe +
- Kayak slalom +
- Archery +
- Handball +
- Judo +

**Montreal** 1976
- Canoe —
- Kayak slalom —

**Moscow** (Unchanged) 1980

**Los Angeles** 1984
- Synchronised swimming +
- Rhythmic gymnastics +

**Seoul** 1988
- Table tennis +
- Tennis +

**Barcelona** 1992
- Canoe +
- Kayak slalom +
- Baseball +
- Badminton +

Atlanta 1996

Softball +
Mountain bike +
Beach volleyball +

Sydney 2000

Triathlon +
Trampoline +
Taekwondo +

Athens (Unchanged) 2004

Beijing 2008

Cycling BMX + — Greco-Roman Wrestling

London 2012

— Baseball
— Softball

Rio 2016

Golf +
Rugby 7s +

103

# Top caps

The most capped international rugby union players, and the percentage of matches they've won

139

Philippe Sella
111 caps
France 1982–1995
70 wins: 63.06%

Victor Matfield
110 caps
South Africa 2001–11
69 wins: 62.73%

George Smith
110 caps
Australia 2000–2009
66 wins: 60%

John Smit
111 caps
South Africa 2000–2011
69 wins: 62.16%

Stephen Jones
110 caps
Wales/Lions 1998–2011
44 wins: 40%

Chris Paterson
109 caps
Scotland 1999–2011
43 wins: 39.45%

Gareth Thomas
103 caps
Wales/Lions 1995–2007
51 wins: 49.51%

Alessandro Troncon
101 caps
Italy 1994–2007
33 wins: 32.16%

Martyn Williams
100 caps
Wales/Lions 1996–2010
45 wins: 43.27%

Number of caps

Percentage of wins

**George Gregan**
139 caps
Australia 1994–2007
93 wins: 66.91%

**Ronan O'Gara**
128 caps
Ireland/Lions 2000–2012
72 wins: 56.69%

**Brian O'Driscoll**
126 caps
Ireland/Lions 1999–2012
75 wins: 59.52%

**Jason Leonard**
119 caps
England/Lions 1990–2004
89 wins: 74.79%

**Nathan Sharpe**
116 caps
Australia 2002–2012
68 wins: 58.62%

**Fabien Pelous**
118 caps
France 1995–2007
79 wins: 66.95%

**Richie McCaw**
116 caps
New Zealand 2001–12
102 wins: 87.93%

**John Hayes**
107 caps
Ireland/Lions 2000–11
67 wins: 62.62%

**Keven Mealamu**
102 caps
New Zealand 2002–12
86 wins: 84.31%

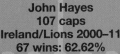

**David Campese**
101 caps
Australia 1982–1996
67 wins: 66.34%

**Stephen Larkham**
102 caps
Australia 1996–2007
68 wins: 66.67%

**Percy Montgomery**
102 caps
South Africa 1997–2001; 2005–08
67 wins: 65.69%

**Mils Muliaina**
100 caps
New Zealand 2003–11
84 wins: 84%

# Sporting celebrations

## Memorable celebrations in sport

Mo Farah
(athletics)
The Mobot

Usain Bolt
(athletics)
The lightning bolt

Frankie Dettori
(horse racing)
The flying dismount

Tommie Smith
and John Carlos
(athletics)
The Black
Power salute

Roger Milla
(football)
The corner flag dance

Alex Ovechkin
(ice hockey)
The hot stick

# Endurance test

**The fastest marathon courses in the world**

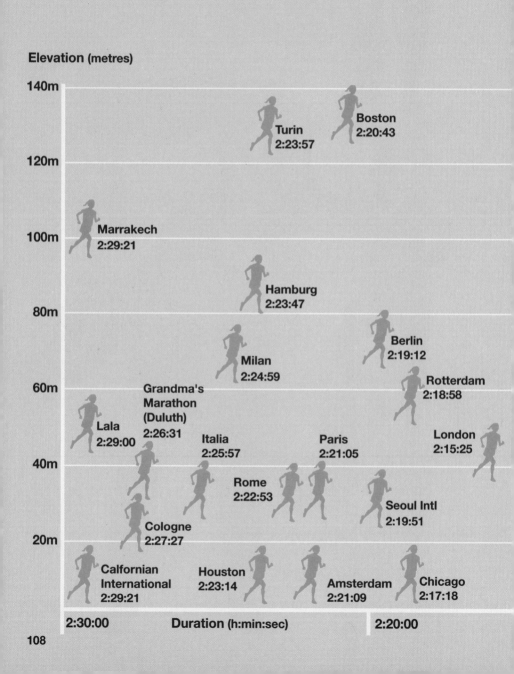

Elevation (metres)

140m

120m

Turin
2:23:57

Boston
2:20:43

100m

Marrakech
2:29:21

80m

Hamburg
2:23:47

Berlin
2:19:12

60m

Milan
2:24:59

Rotterdam
2:18:58

Grandma's
Marathon
(Duluth)
2:26:31

Lala
2:29:00

Italia
2:25:57

Paris
2:21:05

London
2:15:25

40m

Rome
2:22:53

Seoul Intl
2:19:51

Cologne
2:27:27

20m

Calfornian
International
2:29:21

Houston
2:23:14

Amsterdam
2:21:09

Chicago
2:17:18

2:30:00          Duration (h:min:sec)          2:20:00

**Number of runners (2012)**

| | | | | | |
|---|---|---|---|---|---|
| Boston | 22500 | Seoul Intl | 30000 | Turin | 4949 |
| Berlin | 40987 | Amsterdam | 15000 | Milan | 13569 |
| Rotterdam | 16188 | Hamburg | 18000 | Lala | 4500 |
| Chicago | 45000 | Marrakech | 5000 | Grandma's | 10000 |
| London | 37500 | Houston | 13000 | Marathon (Duluth) | |
| Paris | 40000 | Rome | 16000 | Californian | 9000 |
| Italia | 901 | Cologne | 10000 | International | |

Women     Men

Turin
2:07:45

Boston*
2:03:02

*The Boston course doesn't meet the criteria for this to qualify as a world record, so Berlin is officially the fastest marathon

Marrakech
2:06:35

Hamburg
2:05:30

Berlin
2:03:23

Milan
2:07:53

Rotterdam
2:04:27

Lala
2:08:17

Paris
2:05:11

London
2:04:40

Grandma's
Marathon
(Duluth)
2:09:37

Italia
2:08:36

Seoul Intl 2:05:37

Dubai 2:04:23

Cologne 2:08:36

Rome 2:07:17

Calfornian
International
2:10:27

Houston
2:06:51

Chicago
2:03:45

Amsterdam
2:03:35

2:10:00

2h

# Doing the circuit

## 2013 Grand Prix motorcycle racing tracks

### COMMERCIAL BANK GRAND PRIX OF QATAR

Location: Losail Circuit, Qatar
Length: 5.380km/3.343 miles
Longest straight: 1.068km/0.664 miles
Constructed: 2004

### RED BULL GRAND PRIX OF THE AMERICAS

Location: Austin, USA
Length: 5.513km/3.426 miles
Longest straight: 1.200km/0.746 miles
Constructed: 2012

### GRAN PREMIO DE ESPAÑA

Location: Jerez, Spain
Length: 4.423km/2.748 miles
Longest straight: 0.607km/0.377 miles
Constructed: 1986

### MONSTER ENERGY GRAND PRIX DE FRANCE

Location: Le Mans, France
Length: 4.185km/2.600 miles
Longest straight: 0.674km/0.419 miles
Constructed: 1966

### GRAN PREMIO D'ITALIA TIM

Location: Mugello, Italy
Length: 5.245km/3.259 miles
Longest straight: 1.141km/0.709 miles
Constructed: 1974

### GRAN PREMI APEROL DE CATALUNYA

Location: Circuit de Catalunya, Spain
Length: 4.727km/2.937 miles
Longest straight: 1.047km/0.651 miles
Constructed: 1991

### IVECO TT ASSEN

Location: Assen, Netherlands
Length: 4.542km/2.822 miles
Longest straight: 0.487km/0.303 miles
Constructed: 1955

### MOTORRAD GRAND PRIX DEUTSCHLAND

Location: Sachsenring, Germany
Length: 3.671km/2.281 miles
Longest straight: 0.700km/0.435 miles
Constructed: 1996

### RED BULL U.S. GRAND PRIX

Location: Mazda Raceway, USA
Length: 3.610km/2.243 miles
Longest straight: 0.453km/0.281 miles
Constructed: 1957

### RED BULL INDIANAPOLIS GRAND PRIX

Location: Indianapolis, USA
Length: 4.216km/2.620 miles
Longest straight: 0.872km/0.542 miles
Constructed: 1909

### GRAND PRIX ČESKÉ REPUBLIKY

Location: Brno, Czech Republic
Length: 5.403km/3.357 miles
Longest straight: 0.636km/0.395 miles
Constructed: 1987

### HERTZ BRITISH GRAND PRIX

Location: Silverstone, UK
Length: 5.900km/3.666 miles
Longest straight: 0.770km/0.478 miles
Constructed: 1948

### GP APEROL DI SAN MARINO E DELLA RIVIERA DI RIMINI

Location: San Marino, Italy
Length: 4.226km/2.626 miles
Longest straight: 0.565km/0.351 miles
Constructed: 1969

### GRAN PREMIO IVECO DE ARAGÓN

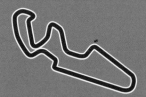

Location: MotorLand Aragón, Spain
Length: 5.078km/3.155miles
Longest straight: 0.968km/0.601 miles
Constructed: 2009

### SHELL ADVANCE MALAYSIAN MOTORCYCLE GRAND PRIX

Location: Sepang Circuit, Malaysia
Length: 5.548km/3.447 miles
Longest straight: 0.920km/0.572miles
Constructed: 1998

### TISSOT AUSTRALIAN GRAND PRIX

Location: Phillip Island, Australia
Length: 4.448km/2.764 miles
Longest straight: 0.900km/0.559 miles
Constructed: 1956

### GRAND PRIX OF JAPAN

Location: Motegi, Japan
Length: 4.801km/2.983 miles
Longest straight: 0.762km/0.473 miles
Constructed: 1997

### GRAN PREMIO GENERALI DE LA COMUNITAT VALENCIANA

Location: Valencia, Spain
Length: 4.005km/2.489miles
Longest straight: 0.876km/0.544 miles
Constructed: 1999

# Cup comparison

## The relative sizes of different trophies in world sport

The Ashes Urn
11cm / weight unknown
CRICKET
England v Australia
First awarded
in 1882

Solheim Cup
48.3cm / 9.1kg
GOLF
USA v Europe
Women's Competition
First awarded
in 1990

UEFA Champions
League Trophy
73.5cm / 8.5kg
FOOTBALL
European Champions
First awarded
in 1967

The 'Salad Dish'
59cm / 11kg
FOOTBALL
German League
Champions
First awarded
in 1949

Larry O'Brien Trophy
61cm / 6.6kg
BASKETBALL
Winner of NBA Finals
First awarded
in 1984

Premier League
76cm / 10kg
FOOTBALL
English League
Champions
First awarded
in 1992

Stanley Cup
89.5cm / 15.5kg
ICE HOCKEY
USA NHL
Champions
First awarded
in 1892

Gentlemen's
Singles Trophy
47cm / weight unknown
TENNIS
Wimbledon Championships
First awarded
in 1887

Vince Lombardi
Trophy
56cm / 3.2kg
**AMERICAN FOOTBALL**
Super Bowl
Winners
First awarded
in 1967

The Calcutta Cup
45cm / 3.2kg
**RUGBY UNION**
England v Scotland
First awarded
in 1879

FIFA World Cup
36.5cm / 6.2kg
**FOOTBALL**
First awarded
in 1974

Copa Del Rey
75cm / 15kg
**FOOTBALL**
Spanish League
Knock-out
Competition
First awarded
in 1976

The Fed Cup
58cm / 15kg
**TENNIS**
International Women's
Team Tennis
First awarded
in 1963

Commissioner's
Trophy
61cm / 14kg
**BASEBALL**
Major League
World Series
winners
First awarded
in 1999

The Ryder Cup
43cm / 1.8kg
**GOLF**
USA v Europe
Golf Competition
First awarded
in 1927

The Web Ellis Cup
38cm / 4.5kg
**RUGBY UNION**
International World Cup
First awarded
in 1987

Davis Cup
110cm / 105kg
**TENNIS**
International
Team Tennis
Competition
First awarded
in 1990

# Bizarre breaks

## Some unusual sporting injuries

### Eye

American footballer Orlando Brown suffered a career-ending injury when a penalty flag was thrown onto the pitch during a game. It hit him in the eye and he missed three seasons. He later sued the NFL for $200 million

### Jaw

Manchester Utd goalkeeper Alex Stepney dislocated his jaw when shouting at his defence

### Shoulder

Basketball player Kevin Johnson shot a match-winning basket, and his team-mate bear-hugged him so ardently in celebration that he dislocated Johnson's shoulder

### Tooth

Major League baseball player Kevin Mitchell chipped a tooth on a chocolate donut that he'd left in the microwave too long. He now boasts a gold tooth

### Collar bone

Clint Barmes, a shortstop with Colorado Rockies, fell and broke his collarbone. A normal if painful injury? Sort of, except he was carrying a large pack of deer meat given to him by a team-mate at the time

## Arm

Pitcher Joel Zumaya had to miss three games after suffering from inflammation in his pitching arm. The cause? Playing too much Guitar Hero on his Xbox

## Back

Sammy Sosa, one of baseball's top home-run hitters, sprained a ligament in his back after sneezing – not once but twice

## Testicles

Ken Griffey Jr found that a box can injure as well as protect. The guard slipped during a game and trapped one testicle – forcing him temporarily out of more than one kind of activity

## Toe

Frostbite in August? Baseball player Rickey Henderson missed three games after falling asleep with an ice pack on his foot. The result was nerve damage in his toe and a red face

## Foot

Spanish goalkeeper Santiago Cañizares severed a tendon in his right foot after he accidentally smashed a bottle of aftershave and a shard of glass penetrated the skin

# The longest season

Length of regular season for different sports

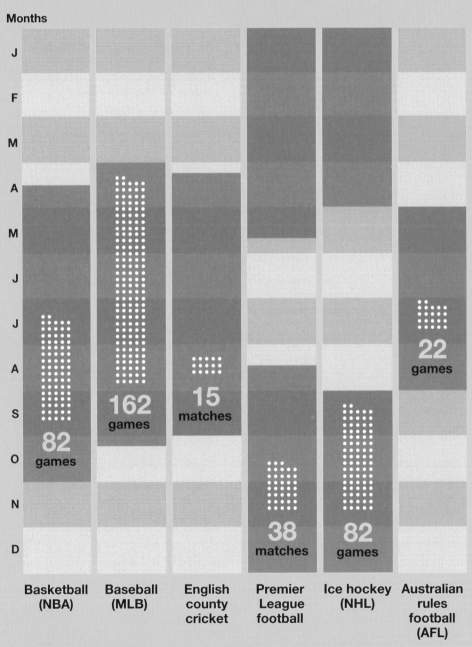

Months

Basketball (NBA) — **82 games**
Baseball (MLB) — **162 games**
English county cricket — **15 matches**
Premier League football — **38 matches**
Ice hockey (NHL) — **82 games**
Australian rules football (AFL) — **22 games**

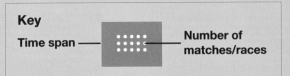

Key

Time span — Number of matches/races

Months

J
F
M
A
M
J
J
A
S
O
N
D

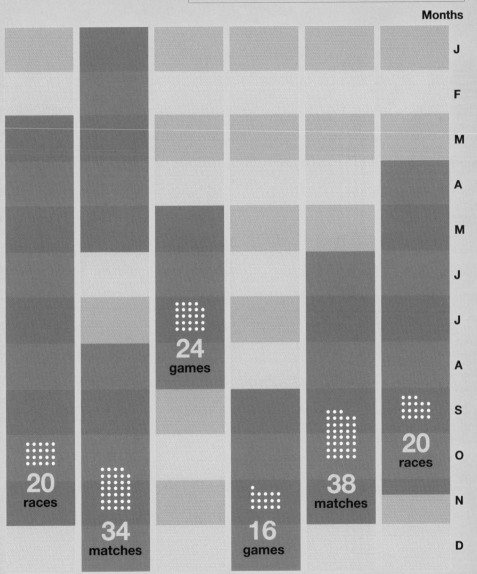

20 races

34 matches

24 games

16 games

38 matches

20 races

Formula One motor racing

Bundesliga football

Australian Rugby League (NRL)

American football (NFL)

Campeonato Brasiliero Série A football

MotoGP

# You need hands

**Umpire signals in cricket, NFL and hockey**

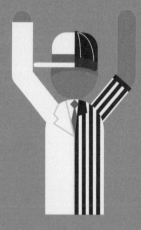

**Cricket: Six**
**NFL: Touchdown**

**Cricket: Bye**
**Hockey: Time started**

**Cricket: Revoke last signal**
**Hockey: Obstruction**

**NFL: Time out**
**Hockey: Time stopped**

**Cricket: Four**
**NFL: Illegal motion**

**Cricket: Dead ball**
**Hockey: Bully**

**NFL: False start**
**Hockey: Ball stopped**
**at penalty corner**

**Cricket: Wide**
**NFL: Unsportsmanly behaviour**
**Hockey: Hit from behind**

# Grand designs

## Important Formula One car designs

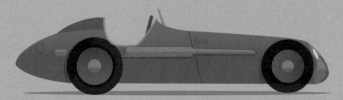

**ALFA ROMEO 158**
Nino Farino won the first Grand Prix in 1950 in this car. The car and its successor took 47 out of the 54 Grand Prix they entered

**COOPER CLIMAX T53**
Jack Brabham won the 1960 Driver's Championship driving the Cooper Climax

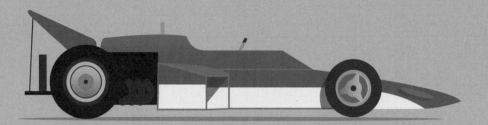

**LOTUS 72**
Two drivers, Jochen Rindt in 1970 and Emerson Fittipaldi in 1972 and 1973, won Driver's Championships in this car

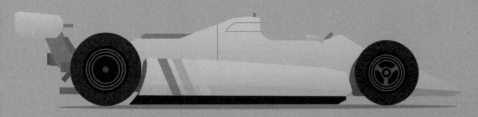

**WILLIAMS FW07**
**Alan Jones drove this to victory in 1980**

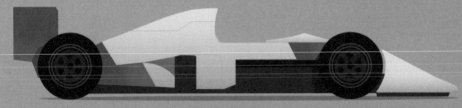

**McLAREN MP4/5B**
**The dominant car of the 1980s. McLaren drivers Alain Prost and Ayrton Senna won 15 out of 16 races in the 1988 season**

**FERRARI F1-2000**
**This car took Michael Schumacher to victory in 2000**

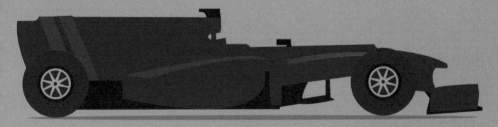

**RED BULL RB6**
**Sebastian Vettel and Mark Webber won 9 out of 16 races in this car in 2010**

# All in a spin

Some of the most famous spin positions in competitive figure skating

**Upright spins**

Corkscrew          Layback          Haircutter

**Sit spins**

Sit spin                    Flying sit spin

**Camel spins**

Camel                      Donut

**Biellmann**        **Shotgun**        **'A' spin**

**Sit spin with twist**    **Death drop jump**    **Pancake spin**

**Butterfly**    **Bent-leg layover spin**    **Side-by-side camels**

# Show me the money!

**Some of the highest-grossing films about sport at the US box office since 1980**

**THE BLIND SIDE**
American football

20/11/09

$255,959,475

**THE KARATE KID**
Martial arts

11/06/10

$176,591,618

**THE WATERBOY**
American football

06/11/98

$161,491,646

**THE LONGEST YARD**
American football

27/05/05

$158,119,460

**JERRY MAGUIRE**
American football

13/12/96

$153,952,592

**ROCKY IV**
Boxing

27/11/85

$127,873,716

**SEABISCUIT**
Horse racing

25/07/03

$120,277,854

**BLADES OF GLORY**
Ice skating

30/03/07

$118,594,548

**REMEMBER THE TITANS**
American football

29/09/00

$115,654,751

**A LEAGUE OF THEIR OWN**
Baseball

01/07/92

$107,533,928

**MILLION DOLLAR BABY**
Boxing

15/12/04

$100,492,203

**42**
Baseball

04/12/13

$95,005,950
(July 2013)

# Making waves

## Common surfboard shapes

12 ─────────────────────────

10 ─────────────────────────

8 ─────────────────────────

6 ─────────────────────────

4 ─────────────────────────

2 ─────────────────────────

0 ─────────────────────────

**FISH**
under 6ft
(1.82m)

Good for
manoeuvring
in small surf

**TOW-IN**
5–6ft
(1.5–1.82m)

For 'towing-in'
to huge swells
by jet ski.
Big-wave,
professional
surfing

**SHORTBOARD**
5.5–7ft
(1.67–2.13m)

Advanced board,
good for tricks
and speed

**EGG**
6–8.5ft
(1.82–2.6m)

Good for
small waves
and beginners

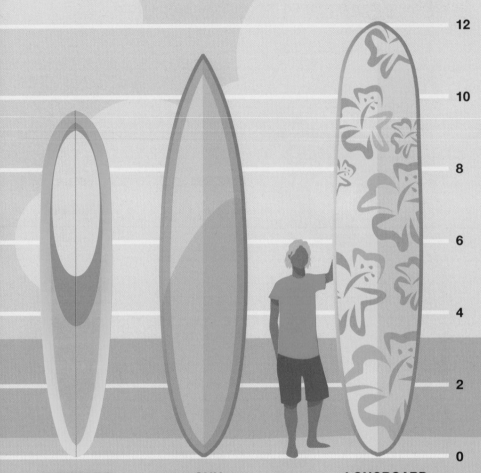

| | | |
|---|---|---|
| 12 | | |
| 10 | | |
| 8 | | |
| 6 | | |
| 4 | | |
| 2 | | |
| 0 | | |

**FUNBOARD**
7–9ft
(2.13–2.74m)

Good for beginners,
more stable than
a shortboard, more
manoeuvrable than
a longboard

**GUN**
7–12ft
(2.13–3.66m)

Stable and easy
to control in large,
faster waves

**LONGBOARD**
9–12ft
(2.74–3.66m)

Graceful and classic,
the original shape

# Seasonal averages

Average season ticket prices of major European football leagues and American Soccer League. Shown in order of ticket value as expressed by cost per home goal

## MLS

Number of clubs in league **19**

USA

COSTS

£⚽
**Per home goal**
**£68.03**

🎟
**Season ticket**
**£1,316**

## SERIE A

Number of clubs in league **20**

ITALY

COSTS

£⚽
**Per home goal**
**£58.17**

🎟
**Season ticket**
**£1,655**

# THE PREMIER LEAGUE

Number of clubs in league

ENGLAND

COSTS

Per home goal | Season ticket

**£25.50** **£865.00**

# LA LIGA

Number of clubs in league

SPAIN

COSTS

Per home goal | Season ticket

**£25.08** **£800.00**

# BUNDESLIGA

Number of clubs in league

GERMANY

COSTS

Per home goal | Season ticket

**£19.45** **£549.00**

# Sporting nicknames

Some curious sporting nicknames and their origins

**Quinton 'Rampage' Jackson**
Mixed martial arts

**Curtis 'CuJo' Joseph**
Ice hockey

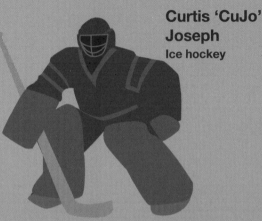

Shortening of first and last names.
Also the name of a killer dog in the novel
of the same name by Stephen King

After 1980s video game

**Gabby 'The Flying Squirrel' Douglas**
Gymnastics

**Kobe 'Black Mamba' Bryant**
Basketball

For her ability to 'fly'
on the uneven bars

In his own words:
"The mamba can strike
with 99% accuracy
at maximum speed,
in rapid succession."

### Earvin 'Magic' Johnson
**Basketball**

### Naim 'Pocket Hercules' Süleymanoglu
**Weightlifting**

One of only three people to have lifted three times their own bodyweight

Coined by a local news reporter after an extraordinary performance

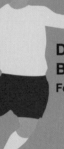

### David 'Goldenballs' Beckham
**Football**

### William 'The Fridge' Perry
**American football**

His size

For his prowess on the pitch and being someone who could do no wrong. Coined by his wife Victoria

### Bruce 'The Flying Doormat' Doull
**Aussie rules football**

The comb-over that flew in the wind

# Cricket cloud

Who are the top run scorers and wicket takers in international Test cricket?

## Run scorers

Ricky Ponting

Sunil Gavaskar

Brian Lara

VVS Laxman

Matthew Hayden

Graham Gooch

Graeme Smith

Jacques Kallis

Steve Waugh

Alec Stewart

Chanderpaul

Virender Sehwag

Allan Border

Rahul Dravid

Shivnarine

Mahela Jayawardene

Sachin Tendulkar

Kumar Sangakkara

Javed Miandad

Inzamam-ul-Haq

Wicket takers

Chaminda Vaas

Allan Donald

# Anil Kumble

Imran Khan

Glenn McGrath

Courtney Walsh

Waqar Younis

Richard Hadlee

Makhaya Ntini

Ian Botham

Malcolm Marshall

Dennis Lillee

# M Muralitharan

Daniel Vettori

Harbhajan Singh

# Shane Warne

Curtly Ambrose

Shaun Pollock    Kapil Dev

Wasim Akram

# Running for office

## Politicians who have competed professionally or represented their country at sport

### 6
**AMERICAN FOOTBALL**

Jon Runyan (USA) Congressman
JC Watts (USA) Congressman
Heath Shuler (USA) Congressman
Steve Largent (USA) Congressman
Tom Osborne (USA) Congressman
Jack Kemp (USA) Congressman

### 5
**ATHLETICS**

Sebastian Coe (GB) MP
Jyotirmoyee Sikdar (India) MP
Bob Mathias (USA) Congressman
Jim Ryun (USA) Congressman
Menzies Campbell (GB) MP

### 1
**BASEBALL**

Jim Bunning (USA) Congressman

### 2
**BASKETBALL**

Bill Bradley (USA) Congressman
Mo Udall (USA) Congressman

### 1
**BODY BUILDING**

Arnold Schwarzenegger (USA) Governor

### 1
**BOXING**

Manny Pacquiao (Philippines) Congressman

### 9
**CRICKET**

Arjuna Ranatunga (Sri Lanka) MP
Sanath Jayasuriya (Sri Lanka) MP
Chetan Chauhan (India) MP
Kirti Azad (India) MP
Navjot Singh Sidhu (India) MP
Mohammad Azharuddin (India) MP
Sachin Tendulkar (India) India's Upper House
Imran Khan (Pakistan) MP
Frank Worrell (Jamaica) Senator

## 1 ICE HOCKEY

Ken Dryden (Canada) Minister of State

## 1 JUDO

Ben Nighthorse Campbell (USA) Senator

## 5 SOCCER

Zico (Brazil) Minister of State
Gianni Rivera (Italy) MEP
Oleg Blokhin (Ukraine) MP
Romário (Brazil) Congressman
Grzegorz Lato (Poland) Senator

## 1 TENNIS

Marat Safin (Russia) MP

## 1 WRESTLING

Jesse Ventura (USA) Governor

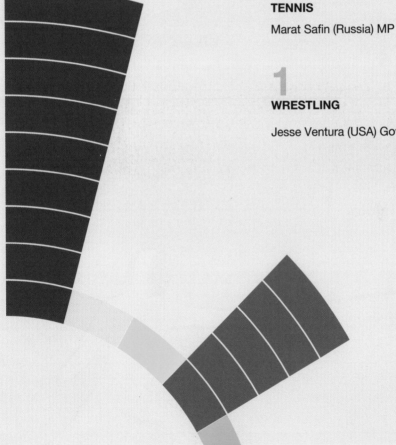

# En garde

## Classic fencing manoeuvres

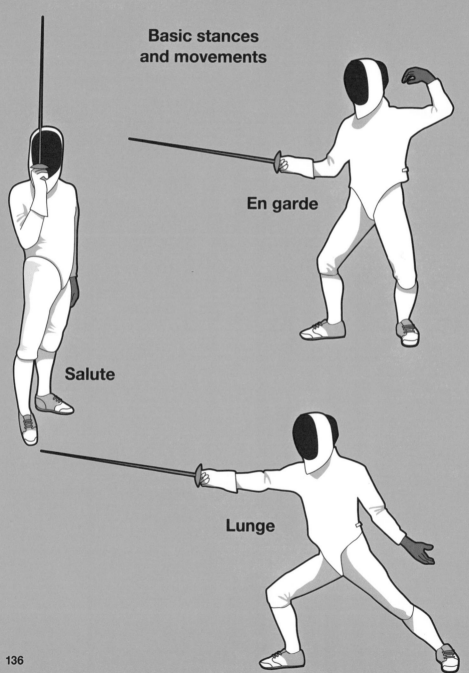

**Basic stances and movements**

En garde

Salute

Lunge

# The nine different foil parries for defence

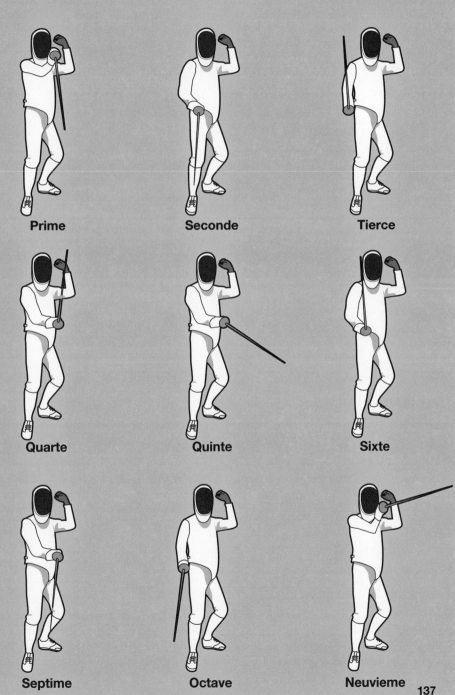

Prime     Seconde     Tierce

Quarte     Quinte     Sixte

Septime     Octave     Neuvieme

# Throwing a whale

Animal-related terms in sport

**ALBATROSS**
A hole played in three shots under par in golf (also a hole in one)

**EAGLE**
A hole played in two shots under par in golf

**TURKEY**
Three strikes in bowling or 30 points in darts or three successive birdies in golf

**DUCK**
An easy shot in snooker and pool or scoring 0 in cricket

**WILDCAT**
Offensive formation in American football

**RABBIT**
A dangerous punch in boxing

**WHALE**
A score of 3 of less in darts

**HOG**
Lines drawn on a curling lane

**FISH**
A score of 9 or less in darts

**BIRDIE**
A hole played in one
shot under par in golf

**FERRET**
Playing the ball
into the hole from
off the green in golf

**SHRIMP**
A very badly hooked
shot in golf

**BUTTERFLY**
A goalkeeping style
in ice hockey

**FALCON**
An 'accidental' knock
to the head using a
ball in rugby league

**DOG**
Missing an easy
shot in pool

**GATOR**
A defensive shot
in volleyball

**SHARK**
A hustler or
good player in pool

# Let's stance

## Some classic karate stances

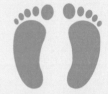

**HEISOKU DACHI**
Feet together stance

**MUSUBI DACHI**
Knot stance

**HACHIJI DACHI**
Open leg stance

**MOTO DACHI**
Foundational stance

**NEKO ASHI DACHI**
Cat stance

**SANCHIN DACHI**
Pigeon-toed stance

**SAGI ASHI DACHI**
**Heron foot stance**

**FUDO DACHI**
**Rooted stance**

**TEIJI DACHI**
**'T' stance**

**KOSA DACHI**
**Cross-legged stance**

**HANGETSU DACHI**
**Half moon stance**

**SHIKO DACHI**
**Square stance**

# Sports illustrated

## The evolution of Olympic swimwear designs

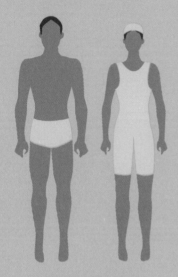

**STOCKHOLM**
**1912**

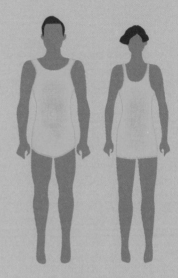

**AMSTERDAM**
**1928**

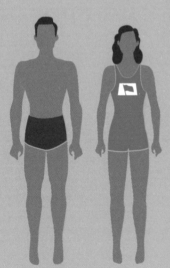

**LONDON**
**1948**

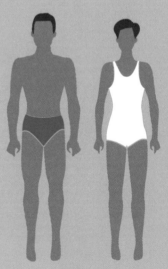

**TOKYO**
**1964**

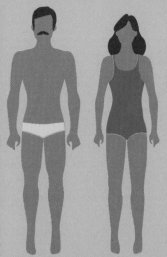

**MUNICH**
**1972**

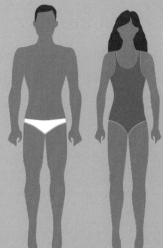

**LOS ANGELES**
**1984**

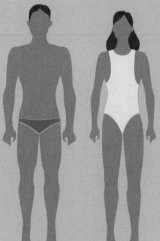

**BARCELONA**
**1992**

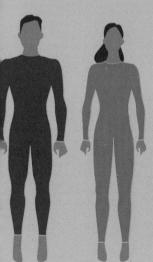

**SYDNEY**
**2000**

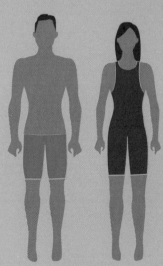

**LONDON**
**2012**

# Rich list

The world's richest sports teams ranked by average first team pay

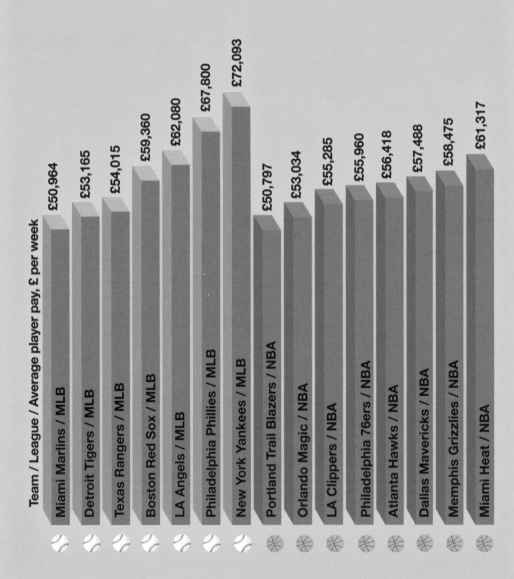

Team / League / Average player pay, £ per week

|  |  |
|------|-----|
| Miami Marlins / MLB | £50,964 |
| Detroit Tigers / MLB | £53,165 |
| Texas Rangers / MLB | £54,015 |
| Boston Red Sox / MLB | £59,360 |
| LA Angels / MLB | £62,080 |
| Philadelphia Phillies / MLB | £67,800 |
| New York Yankees / MLB | £72,093 |
| Portland Trail Blazers / NBA | £50,797 |
| Orlando Magic / NBA | £53,034 |
| LA Clippers / NBA | £55,285 |
| Philadelphia 76ers / NBA | £55,960 |
| Atlanta Hawks / NBA | £56,418 |
| Dallas Mavericks / NBA | £57,488 |
| Memphis Grizzlies / NBA | £58,475 |
| Miami Heat / NBA | £61,317 |

A bar chart showing average player salaries by team/league:

|  |  |
|---|---|
| Boston Celtics / NBA | £62,014 |
| Chicago Bulls / NBA | £62,045 |
| San Antonio Spurs / NBA | £63,514 |
| LA Lakers / NBA | £73,162 |
| Juventus / Serie A | £54,725 |
| Liverpool / EPL | £60,954 |
| Arsenal / EPL | £61,532 |
| Manchester United / EPL | £64,344 |
| Internazionale / Serie A | £66,436 |
| Bayern Munich / Bundesliga | £68,845 |
| Milan / Serie A | £71,143 |
| Chelsea / EPL | £79,197 |
| Manchester City / EPL | £86,280 |
| Real Madrid / La Liga | £90,859 |
| Barcelona / La Liga | £101,160 |

# Snow business

## Basic snowboarding tricks explained

### OLLIE

Ride straight downhill at moderate speed

Crouch slightly, shifting weight to back foot

Lift nose and use tail as a spring

Level board in air and raise knees to chest

### WHEELIE

Ride straight downhill at moderate speed

Crouch slightly and lean backwards

Shift weight to back foot and lift front foot

Return to first position with front foot down

## BUTTER

Ride straight downhill at moderate speed

Lift back of board, pivot off front to turn around

Put board's nose down halfway through turn

Make a ground spin to reach start position

## 50/50 GRIND

Ride towards rail, keeping speed under control

Ollie onto rail, keeping board parallel to rail

Maintain balance and make a small ollie off rail

Land with both feet and then ride away

# Horsing around

Different types of competition at a modern-day rodeo event

Roping

Steer wrestling

Bareback riding

Saddle bronc riding

Bull riding

Barrel racing

The American English term rodeo comes from the Spanish word *rodeo,* meaning 'round up'

Rodeo skills originate from cowboy practices in the USA and Canada

The first professional rodeo took place in Prescott, Arizona in 1888

Rodeo is the official state sport in Texas, Wyoming and South Dakota

Rodeo is banned in the United Kingdom and the Netherlands because of concerns about animal cruelty

# National obsessions

## National sports of different countries

Thailand — Muay Thai

Canada — Lacrosse

Mexico — Charreada

India — Field Hockey

China — Table tennis

Bhutan — Archery

Iceland — Glima

Uzbekistan — Kurash

Russia — Bandy

Bangladesh — Kabbadi

Lithuania — Basketball

Madagascar — Rugby union

Afghanistan — Buzkashi

Belgium — Cycling

Bulgaria — Weightlifting

**Cuba** — Baseball

**Finland** — Pesäpallo

**Argentina** — Pato

**Scotland** — Golf

**Switzerland** — Schwingen

**Iran** — Wrestling

**Japan** — Sumo

**Turkey** — Oil wrestling

**Brazil** — Capoeira

**Hungary** — Water polo

**Sri Lanka** — Volleyball

**New Zealand** — Rugby union

**USA** — Baseball

**Chile** — Chilean rodeo

**Romania** — Oină

# Strike out

## Different pin configurations left after the first bowl in ten-pin bowling

### Dinner Bucket
(bucket if missing 8 pin)

### Double Wood Left
or Sleeper #1

### Double Wood Right
or Sleeper #2

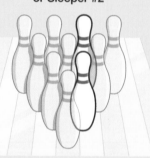

### Baby Split

### Christmas Tree #1

## Greek Church
### or Big Five

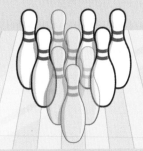

## Goal Posts
### or Bed Posts

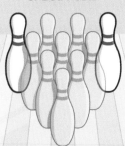

## Dime Store #1

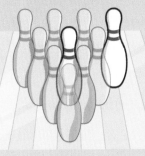

## Big Four

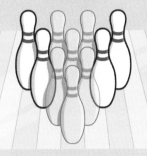

## Lily

## Washout #1

# Climb every mountain?

## The world's most challenging mountains

**Mt Everest**
**8,848m (29,029ft)**
**Nepal**

First ascent: New Zealander Edmund Hillary and Tenzing Norgay, a Nepali sherpa climber, 29 May 1953.
Highest mountain in the world.
The extreme altitude and congested climbing routes are particular dangers

**K2**
**Height: 8,612m (28,253ft)**
**Pakistan/China**

First ascent: Achille Compagnoni and Lino Lacedelli (Italy), 31 July 1954.
2nd highest mountain in the world.
Nicknamed 'Savage Mountain' for its severe weather. It is typically climbed in June, July or August; K2 has never been climbed in winter

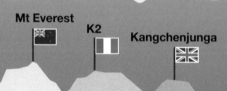

Mt Everest
K2
Kangchenjunga
Annapurna

**Kangchenjunga**
**Height: 8,586m (28,169ft)**
**Nepal/India**

First ascent: George Band and Joe Brown (UK), 25 May 1955.
Most parties stop just below the summit to respect the Sikkemese belief that the top is sacred space

**Annapurna**
**Height: 8,091m (26,545ft)**
**Nepal**

First ascent: Maurice Herzog and Louis Lachenal (France), 3 June, 1950.
An expedition fatality rate of around 40%; the most dangerous 8,000m mountain

**Mt Vinson**
**Height: 4,892m (16,050ft)**
**Vinson Massif, Antarctica**

First ascent: Barry Corbet, John Evans, Bill Long and Pete Schoening, part of a 10-person US expedition, on 17 December, 1966. The most remote, most expensive and coldest of the major mountains to climb

**Baintha Brakk**
**Height: 7,285 metres (23,901ft)**
**Gilgit-Baltistan, Pakistan**

First ascent: Doug Scott and Chris Bonington (GB), 13 July 1977. One of the steepest and rockiest challenges facing mountaineers. 24 years elapsed between the first ascent in 1977 and the second in 2001

**The Matterhorn**
**Height: 4,478m (14,692ft)**
**Pennine Alps, Swiss/Italian border**

First ascent: Edward Whymper and party, 1865 (UK). Four of the party died. From 1865 to 1995, 500 climbers perished on the Matterhorn

**Mount McKinley ('Denali')**
**Height: 6194 metres (20320ft)**
**Alaska, US.**

First Ascent: June 7, 1913 by Hudson Stuck, Harry Karstens, Walter Harper and Robert Tatum.
Also known as 'Denali' from the Inuit word meaning 'The Great One.' At least 120 people have died on McKinley

**The Eiger**
**Height: 3,970m (13,020ft)**
**Bernese Alps, Switzerland.**

First ascent: Charles Barrington with guides Christian Almer and Peter Bohren (Ireland), 11 August 1858. Since 1935, at least 64 climbers have died attempting the north face, earning it the German nickname *Mordwand* – 'murder(ous) wall'

**Mount Fitz Roy**
**Height: 3,359m (11,020ft)**
**Patagonia, Argentina/Chile.**

First ascent: Lionel Terray and Guido Magnone (France), 2 February 1952. Sheer granite faces and particularly treacherous weather make this one of the most formidable mountaineering challenges

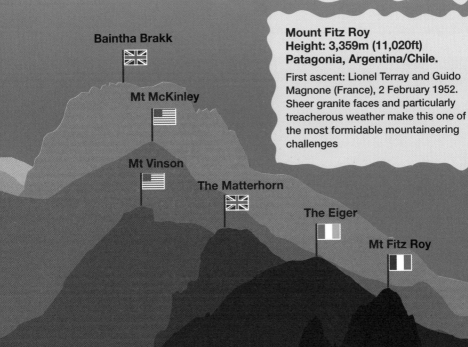

Baintha Brakk

Mt McKinley

Mt Vinson

The Matterhorn

The Eiger

Mt Fitz Roy

# Stat Bowl

## The Super Bowl in numbers

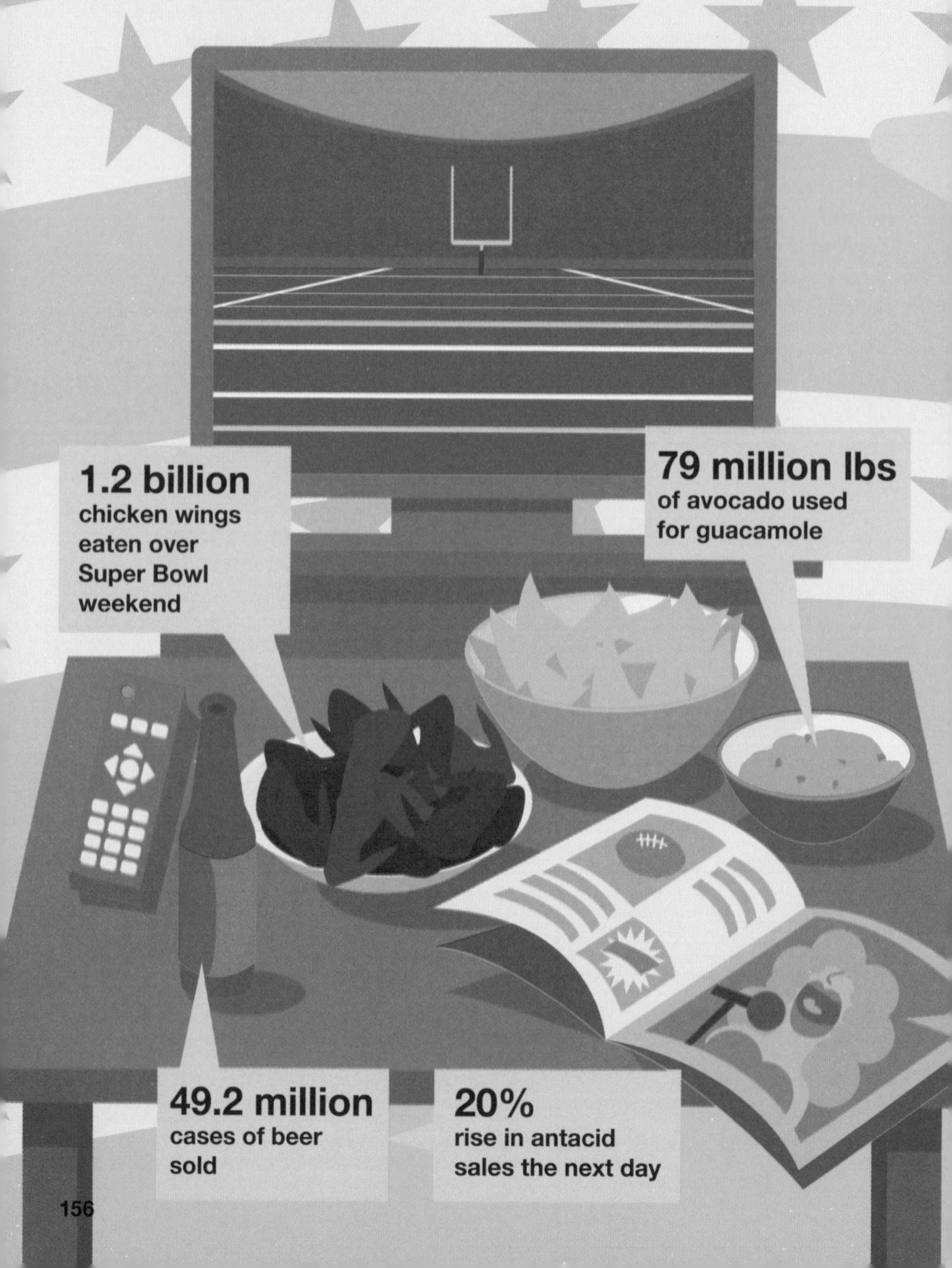

**1.2 billion**
chicken wings
eaten over
Super Bowl
weekend

**79 million lbs**
of avocado used
for guacamole

**49.2 million**
cases of beer
sold

**20%**
rise in antacid
sales the next day

The average cost of a 30-second ad during Superbowl

# $3.8m

There are

# 47.1 minutes
of advert time from kick-off to final whistle

# 7.5m
Americans will buy a new TV for the game

## Half-time entertainers

**2008 Tom Petty and the Heartbreakers**

**2009 Bruce Springsteen and the E Street Band**

**2010 The Who**

**2011 The Black Eyed Peas, Usher, Slash**

**2012 Madonna, LMFAO, Cirque du Soleil, Nicki Minaj, M.I.A., CeeLo Green, Andy Lewis**

**2013 Beyoncé, Destiny's Child**

Lowest-priced ticket (2013)
## $2,253

Highest-priced ticket (2013)
## $13,120

# Contrade

The teams (contrade) that take part in the Siena Palio

PIAZZA IL CAMPO

| TEAM NAME | TRANSLATION | ASSOC TRADE |
|-----------|-------------|-------------|
| Aquila | Eagle | Notaries |
| Bruco | Caterpillar | Silk workers |
| Chiocciola | Snail | Tanners |
| Civetta | Owl | Cobblers |
| Drago | Dragon | Bankers |
| Giraffa | Giraffe | Painters |
| Istrice | Porcupine | Smiths |
| Leocorno | Unicorn | Goldsmiths |
| Lupa | She-wolf | Bakers |
| Nicchio | Shell | Potters |
| Oca | Goose | Dyers |
| Onda | Wave | Carpenters |
| Pantera | Panther | Apothecaries |
| Selva | Forest | Weavers |
| Tartuca | Tortoise | Stonemasons |
| Torre | Tower | Wool combers |
| Valdimontone | Ram | Silk merchants |

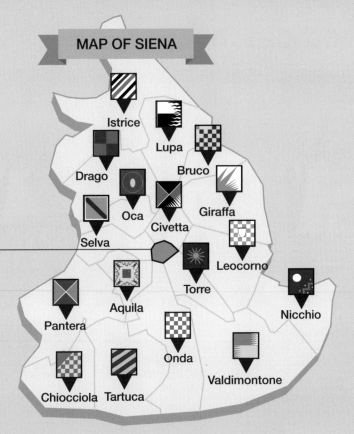

## MAP OF SIENA

Istrice

Lupa

Drago

Bruco

Oca

Giraffa

Civetta

Selva

Leocorno

Torre

Aquila

Nicchio

Pantera

Onda

Valdimontone

Chiocciola Tartuca

| MOTTO | WINS |
| --- | --- |
| From the eagle, beak, the claws, the wing | 24 |
| My name rings out like a revolution | 37 |
| Surely and slowly will the snail win | 51 |
| I see through the night | 33 |
| Fire in my heart becomes flame in my mouth | 36 |
| The higher the head, the higher the glory | 35 |
| I sting only in defence | 41 |
| The arm I bear heals and wounds equally | 30 |
| The arms of Rome, the honour of Siena | 34 |
| It's the red of the coral that burns in my heart | 42 |
| He calls to arms | 64 |
| The colour of Heaven, the power of the ocean | 39.5 |
| The panther roared, the people were afraid | 26 |
| The first forest in the Campo | 37 |
| I welcome strength and consistency | 47.5 |
| Beside the power, the potency | 44 |
| Walls crumble under my horns | 44 |

# A good catch

## Sporting marriages that are lasting the course

**1996**

**Nadia Comaneci**
**Bart Conner**
Olympic gymnasts

**1997**

**Gabrielle Reece**
**Laird Hamilton**
Volleyball and surfing

**2000**

**Kristi Yamaguchi**
**Bret Hedican**
Olympian (figure skating)
and ice hockey

**2001**

**Steffi Graf**
**Andre Agassi**
Tennis

**2003**

**Mia Hamm**
**Nomar Garciaparra**
Olympian (soccer)
and baseball

**2004**

**Misty May-Treanor**
**Matt Treanor**
Olympian (beach volleyball)
and baseball

**2005**

**Kerri Walsh**
**Casey Jennings**
Beach volleyball

**2005**

**Jennie Finch**
**Casey Daigtle**
Olympian (softball)
and baseball

**2007**

**Laila Ali**
**Curtis Conway**
Boxing and NFL

**2007**

**Kim Clijsters**
**Brian Lynch**
Tennis and basketball

**2008**

**Candace Parker**
**Shelden Williams**
Basketball

**2009**

**Mirka Miroslava**
**Roger Federer**
Tennis

# Field of dreams

## Fielding positions in cricket

1. Long stop
2. Long leg
3. Deep third man
4. Fine third man
5. Straight fine leg
6. Deep fine leg
7. Third man
8. Square third man
9. Short third man
10. Short fine leg
11. Square fine leg
12. Deep backward point
13. Fly slip
14. 45
15. Deep backward square leg
16. Deep point
17. Backward point
18. Gully
19. Slips 1–8
20. Wicket keeper

21. Leg slip
22. Leg gully
23. Backward square leg
24. Point
25. Silly point
26. Batsman
27. Short leg
28. Square leg
29. Deep square leg
30. Deep cover point
31. Forward point
32. Silly mid-off
33. Silly mid-on
34. Forward square leg
35. Deep forward square leg
36. Cover point
37. Short cover
38. Short mid-off
39. Batsman (non-striker)
40. Short mid-on

41. Mid-wicket
42. Deep cover
43. Cover
44. Bowler
45. Extra cover
46. Mid-off
47. Mid-on
48. Deep mid-wicket
49. Deep extra cover
50. Deep mid-off
51. Deep mid-on
52. Deep forward mid-wicket
53. Wide long off
54. Wide long on
55. Long off
56. Straight long off
57. Straight hit
58. Straight long on
59. Long on

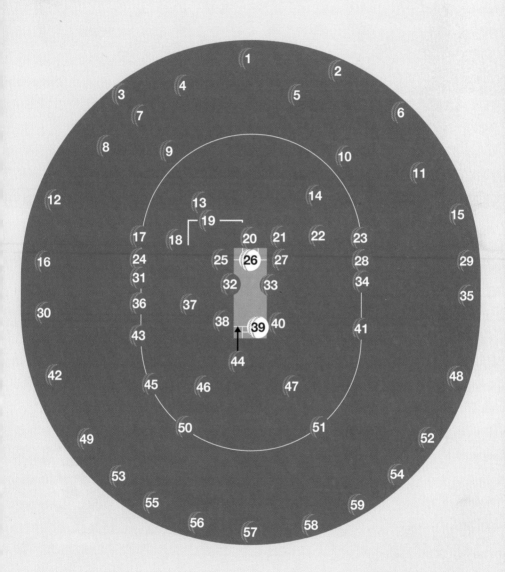

163

# Back of the net

Names of all players who have scored five or more goals in World Cup final tournaments. Size of name reflects number of goals scored

Bergkamp
Szarmach
Eusébio
Müller
Morientes
Wilmots
Völler
González
Basora
Platini
Haller
Míguez
Beckenbauer
Rensenbrink
Probst
Butragueño
Leônidas
Hügi
Milla
Zico
Klose
Seeler
Neeskens
Hurst
Cea
Dahl
Matthäus
Jairzinho
McParland
Krankl
Rossi
Forlán
Kocsis
Lato
Villa
Romário
Morlock
Zsengellér
Nejedlý
Tomasson
Altobelli
Batistuta
Rummenigge
Schiaffino

Jerkovi

Stábile

Pelé

Rahn

Müller

Klinsmann

Rivaldo

Rep

Boniek

Larsson

Salenko

Andersson

Cubillas

Baggio

Zidane

Šuker

Vavá

Skuhravý

Rivelino

Garrincha

Schäfer

Ivanov

Sneijder

Kempes

Sárosi

Podolski

Schillaci

Fontaine

Maradona

Stoichkov

Ronaldo

Careca

Vieri

Hierro

Ademir

Tichy

Donovan

Piola

Bebeto

Lineker

Henry

# In their wake

## The fastest things in and on the water

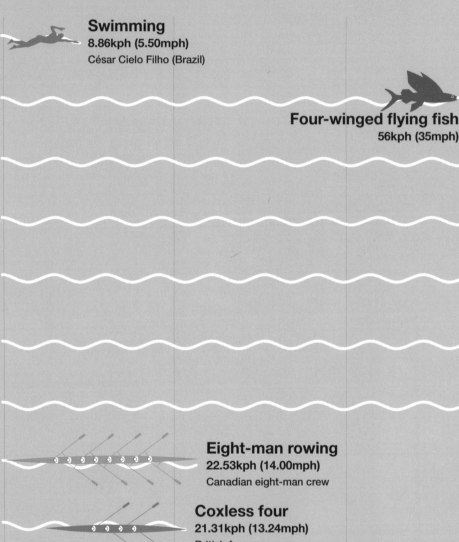

**Swimming**
8.86kph (5.50mph)
César Cielo Filho (Brazil)

**Four-winged flying fish**
56kph (35mph)

**Eight-man rowing**
22.53kph (14.00mph)
Canadian eight-man crew

**Coxless four**
21.31kph (13.24mph)
British four-man crew

**Single kayak**
21.3kph (13.2mph)
Mark de Jonge (Canada)

0 kph                    20                    40

**Great blue shark**
69kph (43mph)

**Bluefin tuna**
70kph (44mph)

**Kitesurfer**
103.06kph
(64.03mph)
Rob Douglas (USA)

**Indo-Pacific sailfish**
110kph
(68.35mph)

**Windsurfer**
90.2kph (56.05mph)
Finian Maynard (Ireland)

60

80

100

110

# Weight ratios

**Champion weightlifters ranked by multiples of bodyweight lifted**

## CLEAN AND JERK

**WEIGHT LIFTED**

**MULTIPLE OF BODYWEIGHT**

197kg — 2.85
Zhang Guozheng — Class 69kg

210kg — 2.72
Oleg Perepetchenov — Class 77kg

218kg — 2.56
Zhang Yong — Class 85kg

233kg — 2.48
Ilya Ilyin — Class 94kg

238kg — 2.27
David Bejanyan — Class 105kg

# SNATCH

| WEIGHT LIFTED | | MULTIPLE OF BODYWEIGHT |
|---|---|---|
| **165kg** | | **2.39** |
| Georgi Markov | Class 69kg | |
| **175kg** | | **2.27** |
| Lu Xiaojun | Class 77kg | |
| **187kg** | | **2.2** |
| Andrei Rybakou | Class 85kg | |
| **188kg** | | **2.0** |
| Akakios Kakiasvilis | Class 94kg | |
| **200kg** | | **1.9** |
| Andrei Aramnau | Class 105kg | |

# Gold country

Gold medal winning countries at London 2012 ranked by ratio of medals to population

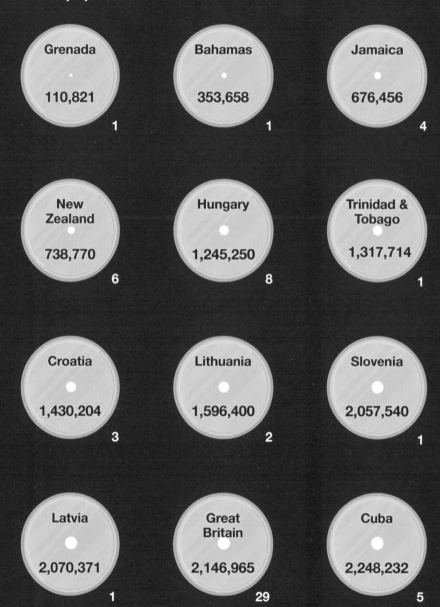

Grenada
110,821
1

Bahamas
353,658
1

Jamaica
676,456
4

New Zealand
738,770
6

Hungary
1,245,250
8

Trinidad & Tobago
1,317,714
1

Croatia
1,430,204
3

Lithuania
1,596,400
2

Slovenia
2,057,540
1

Latvia
2,070,371
1

Great Britain
2,146,965
29

Cuba
2,248,232
5

Kazakhstan
2,388,285
7

Norway
2,502,850
2

Czech Republic
2,626,050
4

Russia
5,960,682
24

United States
6,812,652
46

China
35,456,578
38

Turkey
37,362,134
2

Argentina
40,117,096
1

Colombia
46,475,000
1

Brazil
64,125,498
3

Mexico
112,336,538
1

Key
The smaller the inner circle, the lower the ratio of population to gold medals

Gold medals won

6,812,652

1

Population per gold

# Tour de jersey

**Jerseys worn in the Tour de France and who can wear them**

**NATIONAL JERSEYS**
Can be worn by current
national road race champions
in ordinary stages. National
time trial champions can
wear national jerseys during
time trial stages

**WHITE ON RED
IDENTIFICATION NUMBER**
Most 'fighting spirit'

**YELLOW NUMBER**
Winning team at
each stage

**RAINBOW JERSEY**
Current world champion

**POLKA DOT JERSEY**
'King of the Mountain'
First over the top
of each climb

**GREEN JERSEY**
Highest number
of sprint points

**WHITE JERSEY**
Leading cyclist under
25 years of age
(on 1 January the year
of the race)

**YELLOW JERSEY**
Overall time leader –
the winner

# Charting sports

Songs with sporting titles and how high they reached in the charts

**1** Carl Douglas — Kung-Fu Fighting — UK 1974

**2** Simon & Garfunkel — The Boxer — Netherlands 1969

**4** John Fogarty — Centerfield — US 1985

**7** Queen — Bicycle Race — Norway 1978

**12** Super Furry Animals — Ice Hockey Hair — UK 1998

**14** The Beach Boys — Surfin' Safari — USA 1962

15 Cheech & Chong
Basketball Jones
USA 1973

17 LL Cool J
Mama Said Knock You Out
USA 1991

20 Kraftwerk
Tour de France
Ireland 1983

23 Bruce Springsteen
Born to Run
USA 1975

26 The Intruders
Love Is Like a Baseball Game
USA 1968

38 Peter Gabriel
I Go Swimming
USA 1983

175

# Oceans seven

## Open water swimming's toughest challenges

### IRISH NORTH CHANNEL
Northern Ireland–Scotland
33.7km (21 miles)

Dangers: 12C water,
volatile weather conditions,
jellyfish on calm days

### STRAIT OF GIBRALTAR
Spain–Gibraltar
14.4km (8 miles)

Dangers: very strong cross
currents, heavy maritime traffic

### CATALINA CHANNEL
Santa Catalina island–LA,
California
33.7km (21 miles)

Dangers: water temperature changes
– much colder nearer coast,
unpredictable strong currents

### MOLOKAI CHANNEL
Molokai island–Oahu island,
Hawaii
41.8km (26 miles)

Dangers: very strong currents,
high winds, heat, sharks,
jellyfish

**ENGLISH CHANNEL**
England–France
34km (21 miles)

Dangers: 15C water,
strong currents, very busy
maritime traffic

**TSUGARU STRAIT**
Honshu island–Hokkaido island
19.5km (12 miles)

Dangers: very strong currents,
sharks, sea snakes

**COOK STRAIT**
North Island–South Island,
New Zealand
26km (16 miles)

Dangers: 14C water,
heavy chop, sharks, jellyfish

# Animal invasion

## Animals that have interrupted major sporting events

| | |
|---|---|
| **Animal:** | Pine marten |
| **Sport:** | Football |
| **Teams:** | FC Thun v Zurich (Switzerland) |
| **Incident:** | Marten ran on pitch. Defender's finger bitten |

| | |
|---|---|
| **Animal:** | Owl |
| **Sport:** | Football |
| **Teams:** | Atlético Junior de Baranquilla v Deportivo Pereira (Colombia) |
| **Incident:** | Owl flew on pitch and was hit by the ball. Fatally wounded |

| | |
|---|---|
| **Animal:** | Pigeon |
| **Sport:** | Football |
| **Teams:** | Chelsea v Ipswich |
| **Incident:** | Michael Ballack tried a shot in the warm-up and hit the pigeon. No harm done |

| | |
|---|---|
| **Animal:** | Police dog |
| **Sport:** | Football |
| **Teams:** | Varginha v MG |
| **Incident:** | Dog unharmed after running on the pitch. Ball suffered fatal injuries |

| | |
|---|---|
| **Animal:** | Wasp |
| **Sport:** | Football |
| **Teams:** | Bayern Munich v Bremen |
| **Incident:** | Goalkeeper felled by invading insect |

| | |
|---|---|
| **Animal:** | Cat and duck |
| **Sport:** | Football |
| **Teams:** | Zulte Waregem v Lokeren |
| **Incident:** | Duck followed cat on to pitch. Neither harmed |

**Animal:** Grey squirrel
**Sport:** Football
**Teams:** Villarreal v Arsenal
**Incident:** The squirrel ran in front of Diego Forlan but the Uruguayan still wouldn't pass

**Animal:** Cow
**Sport:** Football
**Teams:** Polish league teams
**Incident:** Cow ran across the pitch. Milked the applause and no one got hurt

**Animal:** Cat
**Sport:** Football
**Teams:** Liverpool v Spurs
**Incident:** The modern legend that is the Anfield Cat. Scampered on, played about, sat down. Left

**Animal:** Jack Russell
**Sport:** International football
**Teams:** Ireland v Australia
**Incident:** Dog tackles player and dribbles ball into touch

**Animal:** Baboon
**Sport:** Golf
**Teams:** Sun City Pro Am, South Africa
**Incident:** Baboon outrages Club members by running across 15th green

**Animal:** Sheep
**Sport:** Cycling
**Teams:** Tour de France
**Incident:** A flock paused on the side of the road on an ascent in the Pyrenees before ambling across in front of the peloton

**Animal:** Kangaroo
**Sport:** Touring Car Race
**Teams:** Bathurst 1000 Australia
**Incident:** Hopped all over the track in front of the cars. No one hurt

**Animal:** Bat
**Sport:** Basketball
**Teams:** San Antonio Spurs v Sacramento
**Incident:** A bat interrupted the game. Manu Ginóbili slamdunked the invader. Bat deceased

# Sun blocks

Beach volleyball moves

## HITS

**Cobra**
Fingers extended,
ball poked with fingertips

**Dig**
Passing the ball with
forearms together,
pushing up

**Kong**
A one-handed block,
often last minute

**Flipper**
Back of hand used
in flipping motion

**Pancake**
'Digging' the ball,
hand flat on floor,
palm down

# HAND SIGNALS

The server's partner will secretly signal the manoeuvre that one of the team will perform to 'block' their opponents' response to the serve

These are some common hand signals:

**One finger**
**Blocker will block**
**a line attack**

**Two fingers**
**Blocker will block**
**an angle attack**

**Open hand**
**Blocker will 'block'**
**shot; partner must**
**defend**

**Closed fist**
**No block –**
**defend with partner**

**Pointing finger**
**Indicates which**
**opponent to serve to**

# Check ID

## The youngest chess players to become grandmasters

**Sergey Karjakin**
Ukraine 2002
12 years, 7 months

**1**

**Parimarjan Negi**
India 2006
13 years, 4 months,
22 days

**2**

**Magnus Carlsen**
Norway 2004
13 years, 4 months,
27 days

**3**

**Wei Yi**
China 2013
13 years, 8 months,
23 days

**4**

**Bu Xiangzhi**
China 1999
13 years, 10 months,
13 days

**5**

**Richárd Rapport**
Hungary 2010
13 years, 11 months,
6 days

**6**

**Teimour Radjabov**
Azerbaijan 2001
14 years, 14 days

**7**

**Ruslan Ponomariov**
Ukraine 1997
14 years, 17 days

**8**

**Wesley So**
Philippines 2007
14 years, 1 month,
28 days

**9**

**Étienne Bacrot**
**France 1997**
**14 years, 2 months**

**10**

**Jorge Cori**
**Peru 2009**
**14 years, 2 months**

**11**

**Illya Nyzhnyk**
**Ukraine 2008**
**14 years, 3 months,**
**2 days**

**12**

**Maxime Vachier-Lagrave**
**France 2005**
**14 years, 4 months**

**13**

**Péter Lékó**
**Hungary 1994**
**14 years, 4 months,**
**22 days**

**14**

**Hou Yifan**
**China 2007**
**14 years, 6 months,**
**16 days**

**15**

**Anish Giri**
**Netherlands 2009**
**14 years, 7 months,**
**2 days**

**16**

**Yuriy Kuzubov**
**Ukraine 2004**
**14 years, 7 months,**
**12 days**

**17**

**Dariusz Swiercz**
**Poland 2009**
**14 years, 7 months,**
**29 days**

**18**

# Synchronicity

## Key synchronised swimming moves

Tub

Split

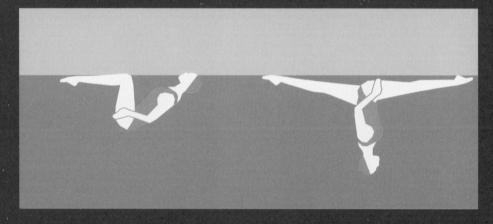

Side fishtail

Ballet leg double

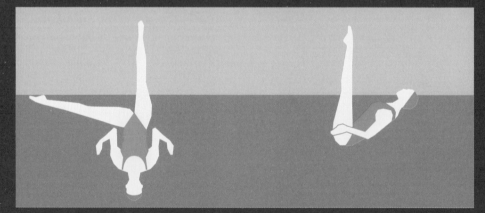

## Flamingo

## Crane

## Knight

## Vertical

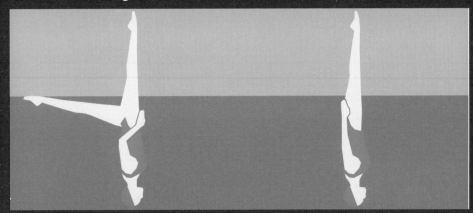

## The dolphin

## Front pike

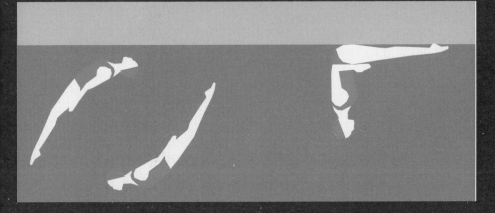

# Sporting siblings

The most successful sporting brothers and sisters
in different sports

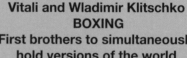

**Vitali and Wladimir Klitschko
BOXING**
First brothers to simultaneously
hold versions of the world
heavyweight championship

**Serena and Venus Williams
TENNIS**
97 tournament wins
between them

**Jim and John Harbaugh
AMERICAN FOOTBALL**
First sibling coaches
to face each other
at the Super Bowl

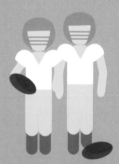

**Michael and Ralf Schumacher
FORMULA ONE**
97 grand prix wins between them

**Peyton and Eli Manning
AMERICAN FOOTBALL**
First brothers to each play
quarterback at a Super Bowl

**Aldo and Nedo Nadi**
**FENCING**
Both Olympic
gold medallists
in all three weapons

**Cheryl and Reggie Miller**
**BASKETBALL**
Both Hall of Fame inductees
Reggie 5 times NBA All-Star;
Cheryl international Hall
of Fame inductee

**Dom, Joe and**
**Vince DiMaggio**
**BASEBALL**
All played professional
baseball

**Bobby and Jackie Charlton**
**FOOTBALL**
World Cup winning brothers

**Rory and Tony Underwood**
**RUGBY UNION**
Played on either wing for
England in the mid-1990s

**Ian, Greg and Trevor Chappell**
**CRICKET**
All played for Australia

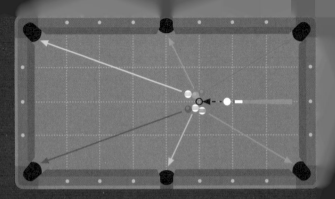

Just showing off

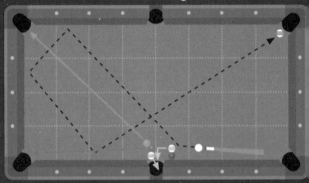

Double shot

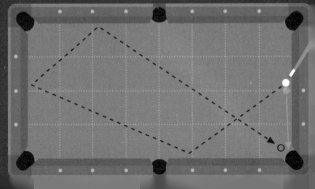

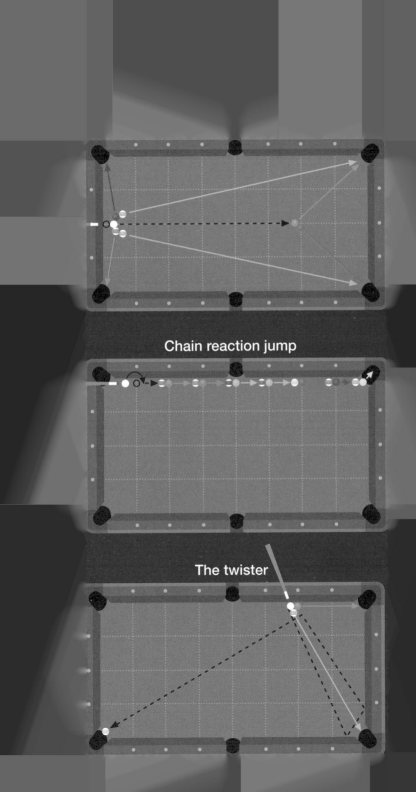

Chain reaction jump

The twister

# Relocation, relocation, relocation

## Teams and franchises that have moved in the US

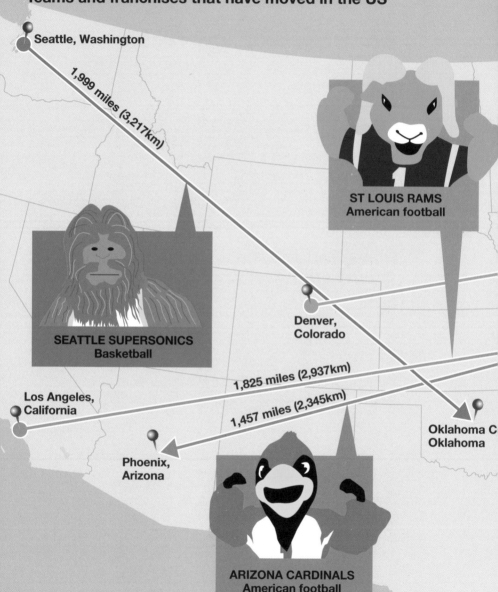

Seattle, Washington

1,999 miles (3,217km)

ST LOUIS RAMS
American football

SEATTLE SUPERSONICS
Basketball

Denver,
Colorado

Los Angeles,
California

1,825 miles (2,937km)

1,457 miles (2,345km)

Oklahoma C
Oklahoma

Phoenix,
Arizona

ARIZONA CARDINALS
American football

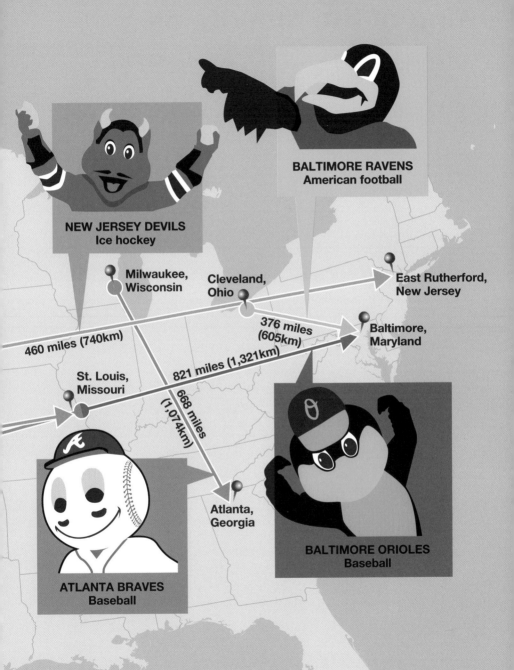

NEW JERSEY DEVILS
Ice hockey

BALTIMORE RAVENS
American football

Milwaukee,
Wisconsin

Cleveland,
Ohio

East Rutherford,
New Jersey

460 miles (740km)

376 miles
(605km)

Baltimore,
Maryland

821 miles (1,321km)

St. Louis,
Missouri

668 miles
(1,074km)

Atlanta,
Georgia

ATLANTA BRAVES
Baseball

BALTIMORE ORIOLES
Baseball

# King of the mountains

Ups and down on the Tour de France course 2013

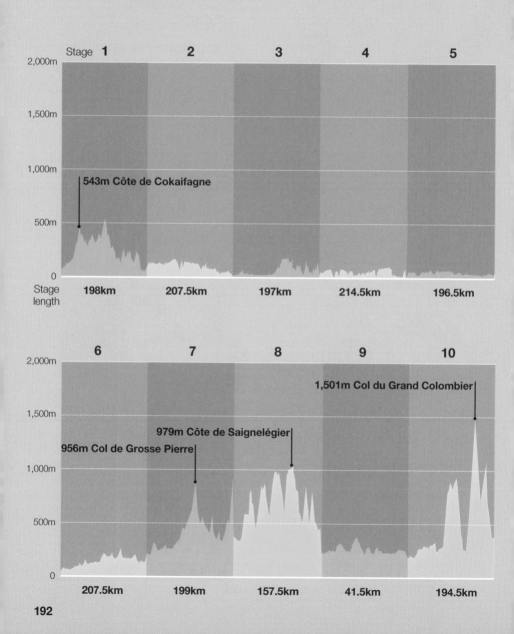

Stage 1     2     3     4     5

2,000m
1,500m
1,000m

543m Côte de Cokaifagne

500m

0

Stage length    198km     207.5km     197km     214.5km     196.5km

6     7     8     9     10

2,000m

1,501m Col du Grand Colombier

1,500m

979m Côte de Saignelégier

956m Col de Grosse Pierre

1,000m

500m

0

207.5km     199km     157.5km     41.5km     194.5km

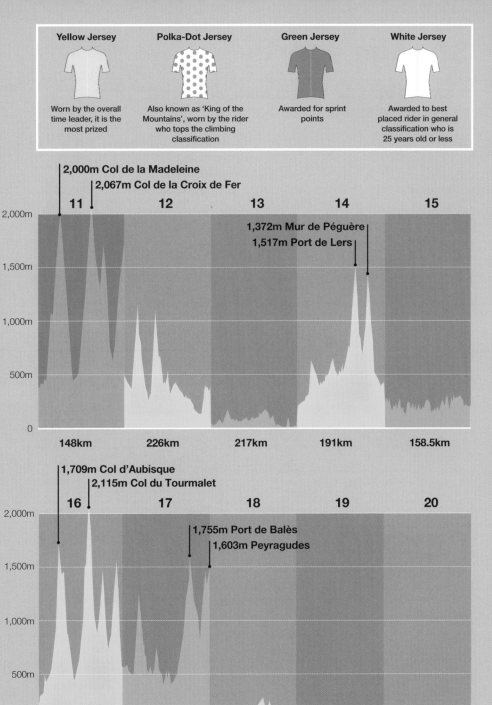

Yellow Jersey
Worn by the overall time leader, it is the most prized

Polka-Dot Jersey
Also known as 'King of the Mountains', worn by the rider who tops the climbing classification

Green Jersey
Awarded for sprint points

White Jersey
Awarded to best placed rider in general classification who is 25 years old or less

2,000m Col de la Madeleine
2,067m Col de la Croix de Fer

11    12    13    14    15

1,372m Mur de Péguère
1,517m Port de Lers

148km    226km    217km    191km    158.5km

1,709m Col d'Aubisque
2,115m Col du Tourmalet

16    17    18    19    20

1,755m Port de Balès
1,603m Peyragudes

197km    143.5km    222.5km    53.5km    120km

# Strange sports

**A glimpse in to the bizarre world of unusual and extreme sporting contests**

**GERMANY**
Fingerhakeln
(finger wrestling)

**UK**
Cheese rolling

**USA**
Lawn mower racing

**SPAIN**
Running with
the bulls

**TURKEY**
Camel racing

**INDIA**
Elephant polo

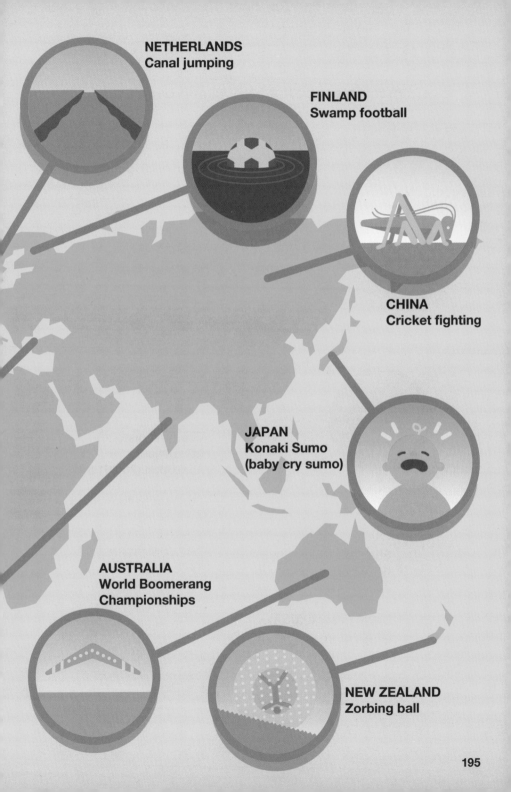

**NETHERLANDS**
Canal jumping

**FINLAND**
Swamp football

**CHINA**
Cricket fighting

**JAPAN**
Konaki Sumo
(baby cry sumo)

**AUSTRALIA**
World Boomerang
Championships

**NEW ZEALAND**
Zorbing ball

# Hot air

Air sports records set by balloonists and parachutists

Greatest distance
in a balloon
40,814km (25,361 miles)

Longest balloon flight
477h 47min

Bertrand Piccard (SUI)
1999

Shortest time around
the world in a balloon
320h 33min

Steve Fossett (USA)
2002

Highest altitude
38,969.4m (127,852ft)

Furthest freefall distance
36,402.6m (119,431ft)

Fastest vertical speed
(without drogue)
1,357.6kph (843.6mph)

Felix Baumgartner (AUT)
2012

Highest balloon altitude
(returning to earth)
34,668m (113,740ft)

Malcolm D. Ross (USA)
1961

Largest freefall
formation
400 parachutists

World Team
2006

Source: Fédération Aéronautique Internationale, FAI – The World Air Sports Federation www.fai.org

197

# On the head

## Iconic international footballer hairstyles

**Bobby Charlton**
England 1958–70

**Fabien Barthez**
France 1994–2006

**Carlos Valderrama**
Colombia 1985–98

**Abel Xavier**
Portugal 1993–2002

**Alexi Lalas**
USA 1991–98

**David Beckham**
England 1996–2009

**Ruud Gullit**
Netherlands 1981–94

**Ronaldo**
Brazil 1994–2011

**Chris Waddle**
England 1985–91

**Marouane Fellaini**
Belgium 2007–

**Roberto Baggio**
Italy 1988–2004

**Kevin Keegan**
England 1972–82

# Ouch!

## Some of the most common sporting injuries

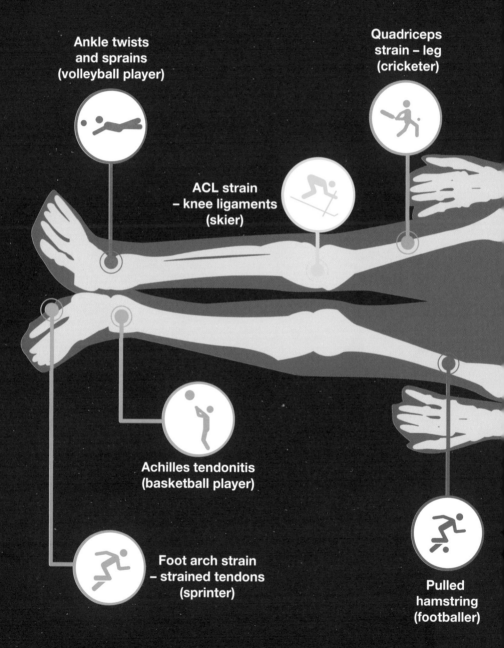

**Ankle twists and sprains (volleyball player)**

**Quadriceps strain – leg (cricketer)**

**ACL strain – knee ligaments (skier)**

**Achilles tendonitis (basketball player)**

**Foot arch strain – strained tendons (sprinter)**

**Pulled hamstring (footballer)**

Back pain
(weightlifter)

Tennis elbow
(tennis player)

Frozen shoulder
(swimmer)

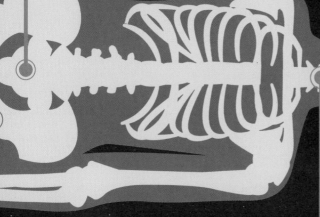

Hip bursitis
– upper thigh
(cyclist)

Neck muscle pain
(tennis player)

# Having a fling

## The main contests which constitute Highland games events

### Scottish hammer throw
Round metal ball is 16lb or 22lb
(7.26kg or 9.98kg) for men,
12lb or 16lb (5.44kg or 7.26kg)
for women

### Stone put
16–26lb (7.26–11.8kg) for men
or 8–18lb (3.63–8.16kg) for women

### Sheaf toss
Pitchfork used to toss 16lb (7.26kg)
bag of straw over horizontal bar. Three
attempts at each successive height

### Weight over the bar
Three attempts at one-handed throw of weight over each successive height

### Caber toss
Aim for a '12 o'clock' toss, where the caber lands and rests vertically in front of the thrower

### Weight throw
Steel or lead weight is 28lb (12.7kg) or 56lb (25.4kg) for men. For all female athletes, the weights are 14lb (6.35kg) or 28lb (12.7kg)

### Maide Leisg ('Lazy stick')
Trial of strength involving two seated competitors pulling on a stick. Whoever levers his opponent off the ground is the winner

# Wrestling masks

## Famous masked wrestlers

### ABYSS

| | |
|---|---|
| Name: | Christopher J Parks |
| Born: | 1973 |
| Height: | 6ft 8in (203cm) |
| Weight: | 350lb (160kg) |
| Debut: | 1995 |

### BATTLE KAT

| | |
|---|---|
| Name: | Dean R Peters |
| Born: | 1958 |
| Height: | 5ft 10in (178cm) |
| Weight: | 220lb (100kg) |
| Debut: | 1984 |

### BLACK BLOOD

| | |
|---|---|
| Name: | Billy Jack Haynes |
| Born: | 1953 |
| Height: | 6ft 3in (191cm) |
| Weight: | 245lb (112kg) |
| Debut: | 1982 |

### BLITZKRIEG

| | |
|---|---|
| Name: | Jay Ross |
| Born: | 1974 |
| Height: | 5ft 6in (168cm) |
| Weight: | 179lb (81kg) |
| Debut: | 1994 |

### BLACK CAT

| | |
|---|---|
| Name: | Victor Mar Manuel |
| Born: | 1954 |
| Height: | 5ft 11in (180cm) |
| Weight: | 220lb (100kg) |
| Debut: | 1977 |

### BLUE DEMON

| | |
|---|---|
| Name: | Alejandro Muñoz Moreno |
| Born: | 1922 |
| Height: | Unknown |
| Weight: | Unknown |
| Debut: | 1948 |

### KANE

| | |
|---|---|
| Name: | Glenn Thomas Jacobs |
| Born: | 1967 |
| Height: | 7ft 0in (213cm) |
| Weight: | 323lb (147kg) |
| Debut: | 1992 |

### CURRY MAN

| | |
|---|---|
| Name: | Daniel Christopher Covell |
| Born: | 1970 |
| Height: | 6ft 0in (183cm) |
| Weight: | 232lb (105kg) |
| Debut: | 1993 |

## MR AMERICA
## (HULK HOGAN)

Name: Terry Gene Bollea
Born: 1953
Height: 6ft 7in (201cm)
Weight: 302lb (137kg)
Debut: 1979

## ULTIMO DRAGON

Name: Yoshihiro Asai
Born: 1966
Height: 5ft 8in (173cm)
Weight: 230lb (104kg)
Debut: 1987

## THE PATRIOT

Name: Del Wilkes
Born: 1961
Height: 6ft 5in (196cm)
Weight: 275lb (125kg)
Debut: 1990

## THE HURRICANE

Name: Gregory Helms
Born: 1974
Height: 6ft 0in (183cm)
Weight: 215lb (98kg)
Debut: 1991

## THE BLUE BLAZER

Name: Owen Hart
Born: 1965
Height: 5ft 10in (178cms)
Weight: 227lb (103kg)
Debut: 1986

## MANKIND

Name: Mick Foley
Born: 1965
Height: 6ft 2in (188cm)
Weight: 287lb (130kg)
Debut: 1986

## REY MYSTERIO

Name: Oscar Gutierrez
Rubio
Born: 1974
Height: 5ft 6in (168cm)
Weight: 175lb (79kg)
Debut: 1989

## KENDO NAGASAKI

Name: Peter Thornley
Born: 1946
Height: 6ft 2in (188cm)
Weight: 210lb (95kg)
Debut: 1964

# Top dollar

## The highest net worth individuals in their respective sports

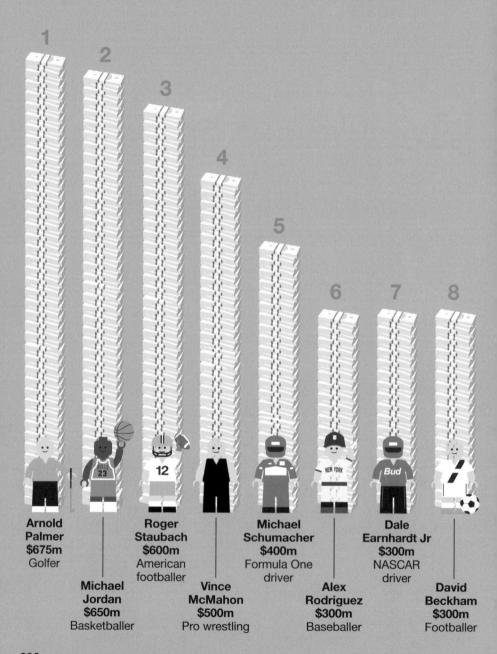

1 Arnold Palmer $675m Golfer

Michael Jordan $650m Basketballer

3 Roger Staubach $600m American footballer

Vince McMahon $500m Pro wrestling

5 Michael Schumacher $400m Formula One driver

6 Alex Rodriguez $300m Baseballer

7 Dale Earnhardt Jr $300m NASCAR driver

8 David Beckham $300m Footballer

After Maria Sharapova ($29 million), the highest-paid female athletes in the world are also tennis players: Li Na with $18.4 million of earnings in 2013 and Serena Williams with $16.3 million

 Basketballer Dwyane Wade reportedly took an $18 million pay cut to allow his team (Miami Heat) to bring in LeBron James and Chris Bosh

 Baseballer Johan Santana signed a six-year contract with the New York Mets for $137.5 million in 2008, and has been injured for every season since

 The most valuable current endorsement deal is worth $260 million, between basketballer Derrick Rose of the Chicago Bulls and Adidas

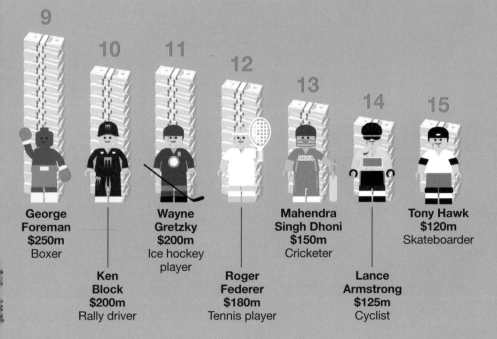

9

10

11

12

13

14

15

**George Foreman $250m** Boxer

**Ken Block $200m** Rally driver

**Wayne Gretzky $200m** Ice hockey player

**Roger Federer $180m** Tennis player

**Mahendra Singh Dhoni $150m** Cricketer

**Lance Armstrong $125m** Cyclist

**Tony Hawk $120m** Skateboarder

Quercus Editions Ltd
55 Baker Street
7th Floor, South Block
London
W1U 8EW

First published in 2014

A catalogue record of this book is available from the
British Library

UK and associated territories: ISBN 978 1 78206 140 3

Printed and bound in Portugal

10 9 8 7 6 5 4 3 2 1

## About the Authors

Martin and Simon Toseland are brothers who have
written successfully on a wide range of subjects, and
as ghostwriters for TV celebrities. This is their second
infographic book for Quercus. Simon plays football for
Bongo Chipolata FC in Bristol; Martin runs with the W4
Harriers in London.

## Acknowledgements

Thanks to Mark Bryson and Jesse Brown for their
graphic design.